50 ways

to manage stress

Stella Cottrell

macmillan
international
HIGHER EDUCATION

RED GLOBE
PRESS

First published 2019 by
RED GLOBE PRESS

Red Globe Press in the UK is an imprint of Springer Nature Limited, registered in England, company number 785998, of 4 Crinan Street, London, N1 9XW.

Red Globe Press® is a registered trademark in the United States, the United Kingdom, Europe and other countries.

ISBN 978–1–352–00579–0 paperback

This book is printed on paper suitable for recycling and made from fully managed and sustained forest sources. Logging, pulping and manufacturing processes are expected to conform to the environmental regulations of the country of origin.

A catalogue record for this book is available from the British Library.

A catalog record for this book is available from the Library of Congress.

Contents

Acknowledgements   vi
About this book   viii
How to use this book   ix
Shape new habits and ways of thinking   x
What is stress?   xi
Why is stress an important issue for students?   xiii
Levels and causes of student stress   xv
Other typical causes of stress   xvi
The effects of prolonged stress   xvii
Vicious cycle of stress   xix
Virtuous cycle of stress   xx
The potential negative effects of stress   xxi
Your own experience of stress   xxii
Using advice and support services   xxiii

50 Ways   **2–103**

Habits shaper: Track your good intentions   104
My progress so far   106
List of 20+ things I appreciate, enjoy or am grateful for ...   108
Where to find out more   110
References and bibliography   114
Index   121
Notes   125

50 Ways

1.	Appreciate 'helpful stress'	2
2.	Harness the benefits of stress	4
3.	Know the signs of excess stress	6
4.	Recognise your own stress triggers	10
5.	Take signs of stress seriously	12
6.	Take charge!	14
7.	Get physical!	16
8.	Talk it through!	18
9.	Get enough (good) sleep	20
10.	Combat homesickness	22
11.	Laugh more!	24
12.	Get well organised	26
13.	Practise mindfulness	28
14.	Get outdoors into nature	30
15.	Watch nature on screen	32
16.	Know your limits	34
17.	Start the day right!	36
18.	Make time work for you	38
19.	Get social!	40
20.	Take stress out of meeting new people	42
21.	Music to your ears!	44
22.	Park your troubles!	46
23.	Create a realistic study schedule	48

24. Change scene and break routine   50

25. Relax with breathing exercises   52

26. Develop good study skills and habits   54

27. Write it out   56

28. Sort your finances   58

29. Take a walk!   60

30. Eat good mood food   62

31. Devise a good exam strategy   64

32. Manage your 'mind exposure'   66

33. Relax jaw and fists   68

34. Avoid task-switching stress   70

35. Benefit from the power of touch   72

36. Trigger the 'happy' chemicals   74

37. Reduce the pressure on assignment deadlines   76

38. Make decisions   78

39. Accept your emotions   80

40. Change your relationship with social media   82

41. Express yourself creatively   84

42. Help someone else   86

43. Befriend your mistakes   88

44. Cultivate a balanced perspective   90

45. Have a good cry!   92

46. Accept yourself   94

47. Use relaxation techniques   96

48. Create a calming sanctuary   98

49. Recharge your energies   100

50. Enjoy a little distraction   102

Acknowledgements

I would like to acknowledge my warmest thanks to those involved in the production of this book, especially Georgia Park and Amy Brownbridge for producing books within the series; Jayne Martin-Kaye for text design; Barbara Wilson for copyediting; Genevieve Friar for proofreading; and Helen Caunce for her oversight and support. I am especially grateful to Claire Dorer and Georgia Park for the innumerable tasks they have undertaken to enable the production of the series, their care over the details and their generous encouragement and goodwill.

"Rollercoaster" icon by Straw Dog Design, p. xi; "Blood pressure" icon by Amy Morgan, p. xii; "Graduation" icon by Rediffusion, p. xiv; "Stressed" icon by Nicole Hammond, p. xix; "Meditation" icon by Gan Khoon Lay, p. xx; "Magnifying glass" icon by Nesi Ratna Nilasari, p. 7; "Write" icon by Arthur Shlain, p. 11; "Chat bubble" icon by Popular, pp. 11, 19, 41; "Ordered list" icon by Wireform, p. 13; "Vacuum cleaner" icon by Nociconist, p. 17; "Gardening" icon by Milinda Courey, p. 17; "Walking" icon by Adrien Coquet, pp. 17, 19; "Sleeping" icon by Adrien Coquet, p. 20; "Home" icon by Numero Uno, p. 23; "Guitar" icon by Adrien Coquet, pp. 23, 85; "Potted plant" icon by Alex Muravev, p. 23; "Family" icon by Gan Khoon Lay, p. 23; "Couch" icon by Diego Naive, p. 23; "Smile" icon by Ester Barbato, p. 25; "Radio" icon by Genius Icons, p. 25; "Comic book" icon by Carlo Cariño, p. 25; "Meditation" icon by Juan Pablo Bravo, p. 29; "Sun" icon by Oksana Latysheva, p. 31; "Countryside" icon by Symbolon, p. 31; "Fish" icon by Yasminvisible, p. 33; "Seaweed" icon by Cristiano Zoucas, p. 33; "Timepiece" icon by ProSymbols, p. 36; "Clock" icon by Bmijnlieff, p. 39; "Queue" icon by Gan Khoon Lay, p. 41; "Parking" icon by Chameleon Design, p. 46; "Coffee" icon by Jacob Halton, p. 51; "Exterior window" icon by Ben Davis, p. 51; "Bubbles" icon by Chiara Rossi, pp. 52, 53; "Study" icon by Susannanova, p. 55; "Study" icon by Adrien Coquet, p. 55; "Piggy bank" icon by LAFS, p. 59; "Credit cards" icon by Jeff, p. 59; "Cabbage" icon by Icon 54, p. 63; "Eggs" icon by Milinda Courey, p. 63; "Fish" icon by Vectors Market, p. 63; "Teapot" icon by David, p. 63; "Cacao" icon by Mariya Zola, p. 63; "Relax" icon by Adrien Coquet, p. 68; "Yawn" icon by Lance Hancock, p. 69; "Check" icon by Adrien Coquet, p. 71; "Cat" icon by B Farias, p. 73; "Signpost" icon by Santri Icon; "Design" icon by

Andrew Nolte, p. 85; "Art design" icon by Delwar Hossain, p. 85; "Camera" icon by Bmijnlieff, p. 85; "Lightbulb" icon by Davo Sime, p. 85; "First aid" icon by Gregor Cresnar, p. 87; "Balance" icon by Delwar Hossain, p. 91; "Yoga" icon by Lluisa Iborra, p. 97; "Candles" icon by Hopkin, p. 99; "Plant" icon by Gemma Evans, p. 99; "Lotus tea" by Vectors Market, p. 99; all from the Noun Project (www.thenounproject.com).

About this book

This book suggests 50 Ways to manage stress whilst a student. It includes:

- Ways to use, and benefit from, stress

- Ways to prevent excess stress (at least for more of the time!)

- Ways to cope when over-stressed

- Ways to reduce excess stress

Many of the suggestions involve an element of self-nurturing, relaxation or fun, so can be enjoyable as well as helpful for relieving stress.

Just a taste ...

This is a small book with many big ideas. Each 'Way' is a starting point, offering suggestions of things to do and to think about. Browse these to spark ideas of your own. You may find this small taste is enough in itself to spur you to action – or you can follow up suggestions using the resources recommended.

Map your own route

Stress is a highly personal experience, so use page ix to get started, then select from the 50 Ways to suit your own circumstances and interests. Be adventurous – try out things you might not usually consider.

The 50 Ways series

This series is especially useful for students who want to dip into a book on an aspect of study or student life that is relevant to them at this point in their studies. The 50 Ways books are easy to carry around for a short burst of inspiration and motivation.

This book is not a replacement for specialist counselling, therapies or medical care.

How to use this book

Get started
Begin with the introduction
and Ways 1–5.

Discover
Find out about stress and different things
that people do to use it and to manage it.

Become more self-aware
Find out more about yourself through
trying out different things.

Reflect
Use the mini self-evaluations to focus your thinking. Then
consider possible ways forward suggested by your answers.

Choose
Decide which of the 50 Ways you want to
try out. You don't have to do them all!

Commit
Once you decide to commit to something, put your
whole self behind your decision. Do it!

Shape new habits
Make stress-management a natural part of
your everyday routine. See page x.

Find out more
Follow up using the recommended resources if you wish.
See pages 110–13 or use the reference list to follow
up sources numbered in superscript in the text.

Shape new habits and ways of thinking

Don't wait until you 'feel stressed'

It is easier to try out new things when you feel less under pressure. You can start to reduce stress straight away – just by making a change. Manage stress longer term by developing a repertoire of coping mechanisms. Flip through the book from time to time to stimulate your thinking and stay on top of stress.

Start to shape new habits

The Ways suggested in this book aren't a quick fix for excess stress but, over time, they will help to build confidence and improve your health and well-being. Developing good lifestyle habits can help you to use stress effectively, maintain it at reasonable levels and cope better with new challenges.

- Be active in shaping new habits – and new ways of thinking. Most pages provide opportunities to reflect, choose, decide and commit.

- Put yourself fully behind your good intentions – write down what you intend to do, using the 'I will' boxes. Be selective: you don't need to do this on every page. You can use pages 104–5 to track and monitor new habits you want to form.

- Keep track of your progress. It takes time to form new habits so give it time and keep returning to them. You can use pages 106–7 to track your progress with any of the Ways you try out.

Feeling panic, anxiety or depression now?

If you are feeling highly stressed, anxious, depressed, panicked or are considering harming yourself or others, talk to someone who can help. Don't wait until things get worse.[1,2] See page xxiii.

What is stress?

Stress is the amount of pressure placed on an object or person. Being 'stressed' is a personal response to the pressure of a situation, event or circumstances. Some people can manage a lot of pressure, others less.[3,4] What we experience as a 'feeling' of stress is the result of how our minds perceive pressure: what excites and energises one person is experienced by others as too much pressure. Even 'doing nothing' is relaxing for some but makes others anxious.

It's exhilarating!

I feel excited!

It energises me!

I love the challenge!

I feel scared but I can manage it

I'll like the sense of achievement later!

It's scary but there are things I enjoy about it!

It's too much for me!

I can't keep track of what is happening

I feel out of control

It's too much pressure for me

I feel like I can't cope

It makes me feel upset

I just want it to stop

What excites one person, stresses another

A natural response

Stress has helped us to survive and thrive as a species. Much of what we experience as stress is the result of chemical reactions used by the brain to warn us of potential danger and set in train our 'fight or flight' mechanisms:

- The heart rate increases

- Blood pressure rises

- More adrenaline is released into the blood

- Glucose levels rise to give more energy to fight/run away.

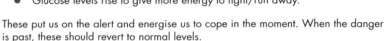

These put us on the alert and energise us to cope in the moment. When the danger is past, these should revert to normal levels.

A helpful energiser

In short bursts, the alertness brought about by the stress response can be useful for study, problem-solving and performance.

Stress inoculation: A learning response

Experiencing a highly stressful situation triggers the brain into action for several hours. This is to help our systems absorb what occurred so we can recognise similar challenges speedily in the future and respond in ways that will enable our survival. Taking on stress in a positive way builds our coping mechanisms and helps us to take on future challenges with less anxiety.[5]

Excitement or stress?

The same chemical combination in our bodies signals both excitement and fear. It is our minds that decide whether we interpret the experience as scary or exciting. Knowing this gives us power over our responses.

Unhelpful sense of danger?

We need our bodies to switch off the stress response and use up excess adrenaline. If we don't need to fight or run away, the adrenaline can hang around in our bodies, leaving us feeling unsettled or 'on edge' or with a sense of nameless dread. Our minds remain on the lookout for supposed threat, searching for potential problems and replaying known worries, keeping us anxious.

Why is stress an important issue for students?

Student life creates its own combination of potential stressors.

Shock of the new

A new course and institution can feel bewildering. It can take time to get used to the change. There is a lot to process, which can be tiring.

Homesickness

Student life can be amazing, but it is hard to be away from familiar people and places. It is natural to feel homesick at times.

Academic challenge

Study is meant to stretch your mind so that you grow academically. Whilst that is good, it can also be unsettling when it feels you are constantly grappling with difficult material and can't get through the work easily.

Workload and grades

Research suggests that students get stressed by the sheer amount of work they have to do.[6] They worry about assignments, exams and getting good grades.

Pressurised deadlines

Meeting deadlines for submitting assignments or being ready for an exam adds to the sense of pressure. As you don't set those deadlines, it can feel as if you have no control at all – but you do!

New responsibilities

For many, it is the first time living away from home, taking care of all aspects of everyday life on their own. That takes some adjustment.

Multiple responsibilities

Many students have jobs, family and caring roles and other commitments that add to their responsibilities and eat into time.

Unstructured time

Having lots of study time to structure for yourself can be disorientating. Things can go wrong if you don't take steps to manage time effectively.

Social pressures

You are surrounded by people you don't know. This can feel lonely or as if you don't 'fit in'. It might seem everyone else has great social networks, even if those are not all that they seem.

Fitting everything in

There are exceptional opportunities open to students: new experiences, work, travel, friends, knowledge, skills, growing as a person. When tired, it might all seem exhausting or too much!

Worry about the future

After being in education for almost all your life, it can be scary thinking of this coming to an end, especially if there are many unknowns about what to do next. It might mean making decisions on matters not yet clear to you, such as work, jobs, careers or where to live.

Money worries

Concerns about loans or debts can be stressful. Students usually have low incomes so they have to be creative in making money stretch.

Student lifestyle

Busy timetables, racing between back-to-back classes, not eating proper meals, staying up all night to study (or party), missing lots of sleep: all these drain physical and mental resources. Tobacco, recreational drugs, alcohol, coffee and sugar don't help stress either!

And students still do well!

All these demands can be experienced as too much pressure or unhelpfully stressful. They are real. They can be tricky – but they don't last for ever. Students do get through them and succeed! It is possible to find ways of easing your stress, managing stress – and to have a great time as a student!

Levels and causes of student stress

A common concern
Students around the world report feeling highly stressed at some time.[7,8,9,10,11,12] For example, in Northern Ireland, 78% of students reported mental health concerns in the past year, stress being an issue for more than four in five of them. Others reported anxiety, lack of energy or general unhappiness.[10] Student stress has been a concern for decades.[13] In the USA, in 2004, over 50% of college students reported being too depressed to function.[14,15] Generally, international students have tended not to report stress or gain support.[16,17,18]

Study-related stress
Study-related worries, such as pressure to succeed, exams, and coping with assignments and the intellectual demands of the course, are the main cause of student stress in many countries – from India to the UK to Saudi Arabia.[9,11,12,19,20] A 2017 study found 87% of new UK students struggled to cope with the academic or social aspects of student life.[9]

Similar concerns
Although causes of stress vary by course, gender and culture,[11,15,19] students worry about similar things: study, relationships, home sickness, family problems, food, accommodation and money.

Age-related stress
It is important to bear in mind that student stress levels are not necessarily any worse than those found in the overall population of young adults. In particular, serious mental disorders tend to be lower amongst students – for example, 12% of UK students compared to 25% of the whole population.[21]

Some common mental health illnesses such as eating disorders, alcoholism, addiction, depression and bipolar disorders tend to appear first during early adulthood. They coincide with the time when many young people are at college or university, so their first experience of such difficulties will be when they are already going through other key life transitions.[22]

Other typical causes of stress

Stress internationally
Feeling stressed is a global phenomenon – similar causes affect people around the world. In India, 90% of people suffer from stress, higher than an already high global average of 86%.[23] Money and work are key causes of stress there. However, India had the best ratings for well-being, too (70.4 compared to a 61.2 global average).

Similarly, high levels of stress are reported in China, where key causes are long working days and high costs of accommodation and living.[24]

In a UK survey in 2018, 85% of adults said they experienced stress regularly. The most common causes were money, work, health, lack of sleep and daily tasks that had to be done.[25]

In the USA, in a 2014 survey of 2500 adults, almost half of these had experienced a stressful event in the past year. Respondents were asked to indicate the kinds of experiences they found most stressful. The results opposite show that nearly two-thirds of causes are related to everyday matters such as health, bereavement, work, family and change.[26]

Typical causes of stress (USA)

Health-related (27%)
Bereavement (16%)
Work-related (13%)
Family events (9%)
Life transitions (9%)
Personal relationships (6%)

These affect students too
Students experience the usual range of factors associated with excess stress, such as money, moving home, bereavement, divorce in the family, relationships and health concerns. If any of these are weighing on your mind now, it is useful to talk it through with someone you trust (Way 8).

The effects of prolonged stress

Whilst some stress is useful, especially in short bursts, prolonged stress affects us negatively physiologically, chemically, emotionally, socially and cognitively. The causes and effects can become mutually reinforcing, making it hard to break a cycle of negative and harmful thoughts and behaviours.

Being 'out of balance'

Excess or prolonged stress puts your system out of balance. Any aspect of life might be affected, depending on the individual. You might notice you are 'not yourself' or not getting things done as before. Or you could perform well at some things but show signs of stress without even realising. Others might notice you have changed, are more irritable, tired, snappy, or neglecting well-being.

Physical effects

These could include:

- Skin problems (acne, eczema, etc.)
- Palpitations; rapid heart beat
- Poor digestion, upset stomach or constipation
- Shakiness; wobbly legs; feeling faint or clammy
- Headaches or migraines.

Physiological effects

- Potentially harmful levels of the hormone cortisol
- Reduced levels of chemicals associated with 'happiness' and well-being, such as serotonin, dopamine and oxytocin
- Suspension of functions such as digestion, tissue repair and the immune system (as these are not needed for immediate 'threats').

Cognitive impacts

- Easily distracted
- Attention drawn to external stimuli and potential threats
- Poorer decision-making, creativity and problem-solving.

Impact on emotions, social life and behaviour

- Difficulties sleeping
- Feeling scared or vulnerable
- Harder to relax or feel calm
- Withdrawing from social networks; spending less time with friends and family
- More likely to abuse alcohol, drugs, food, other substances
- Behaving in ways that are not typical of you/unhelpful to you
- Poorer quality of life
- Weaker sense of well-being.

Impact on study

- Weaker focus/concentration
- Harder to settle down to study and stick with tasks
- Harder to absorb material in class or when reading, and to recall material
- Study tasks can take longer and/or work is poorer quality
- Fear of lower grades/failure.

Impact on thought patterns

- Thoughts get caught up in cycles of worry

- A focus on things that could go wrong
- It is harder to think of a way out of the difficulties
- It can feel as if there is no escape.

Impact on mental health

- Feeling overwhelmed and unable to cope
- A sense of panic or anxiety
- Panic attacks
- Low mood/depression
- Potentially, long-term mental ill-health.

Impact on health

A continued period of high stress can damage health at any age.

- It can weaken the immune system, increasing vulnerability to disease and reducing the ability to fight off sickness
- Over time, high cortisol levels break down muscle, weakening the heart and other organs[27]
- Cortisol can also damage hippocampus neurons, affecting learning and memory.

Vicious cycle of stress

Anxiety; constant worrying; feelings of dread; fear of failure

Little sleep, relaxation or sense of calm

Lack energy. Hard to think, concentrate, or stay focussed

Life feels drained of fun and interest

It all feels too much. You don't act or feel like yourself

Harder to learn, understand and remember

Less time for everything else

Work takes longer to complete well

Virtuous cycle of stress

Feel happier – and more confident that can deal with setbacks

Sleep better. Address challenges calmly

Take more interest in things. Engage more in social life, family, nature, study

Greater sense of self, calm, control

More alert, more energy

More time for everything else

Perform well in the moment

Get things done

The potential negative effects of stress

Stress affects individuals differently. In a survey in the USA (2015),[25] 74% of respondents said it affected their health, 63% said it affected their emotional well-being, whilst stress didn't have that effect on others. Over half of respondents reported difficulties with sleep, thinking, decision-making and concentration, but a large minority didn't have these symptoms or were not aware that they did. In an Australian survey (2015),[28] 70% of respondents said that they used food as a way of managing stress.

The effect on students

Research indicates that stress affects students in multiple ways, directly and indirectly.[29,30] Here are some to watch out for.

- Becoming ill frequently or being unable to throw off illness, if the immune system is weakened by stress

- Engaging in less physical exercise, which in turn affects stamina, weight, health and sense of well-being

- Less effective and efficient study – from reduced ability to focus, concentrate and remember material

- Feeling over-anxious about failure in their studies and lives, or a general sense of dread

- Social withdrawal, isolation and loneliness because they don't have the energy to socialise, or others don't want to socialise with them anymore, or because of having to spend longer to get through their studies.

Your own experience of stress

Experiencing short spells of acute stress?
Many of the causes of student stress are short term, such as being new to university, starting a new class, having an essay or exam to complete, or immediate financial problems. These can feel hard, but they can help you to do well, too. They can seem to last a long time so it is important to bear in mind that they really don't last forever.

Don't notice stress?
Some people don't notice that they are under excessively high levels of stress and so keep going for a long time. That isn't always a good thing, as it can lead to serious long-term impairment of their health. They may also be behaving in ways that are affecting their social lives without them realising, such as being irritable, snappy, dismissive, or withdrawn and neglectful of friends and family. They may also be making poor decisions about their studies and health. If that could be you, be self-aware so that you take proper care of all aspects of your life.

Aware of long-term stress and mental health issues?
It is helpful if you are already aware that you need to take care of your mental health. If your university or college has confidential counselling services, it is a good idea to talk to these early on in order to make a sensible plan for managing stresses that arise from student life and study. Let them know what you think would be useful as support. Make use of the resources and groups available on campus or in the local area.

Using advice and support services

A huge variety of routes

Universities and colleges worldwide vary in the quality of support available, but there is increased awareness of the need to provide good support.[12] Methods vary: lifestyle approaches using sports, art therapy, drama, music, massage therapy, reflexology, meditation or yoga, to medical routes such as talking to nurses, doctors, counsellors, therapists and psychiatrists. In addition, a chat with your personal tutor, year tutor, lecturers or course administrators can be a helpful step in finding the right help and support.

Student services are there to be used

Support staff are used to being approached about everything from loneliness to severe mental health conditions, so you need not be embarrassed to ask for a chat or support. Enquiries and help are normally confidential but ask about this at your first contact.

When to seek out advice and support

- If you feel you need it or that it might help
- If you feel isolated, lonely or homesick and unsure how to handle this
- If life, study or your feelings seem to be getting out of control
- If you are starting to neglect basics, such as eating, socialising, taking care of yourself
- If you abuse food, drugs, alcohol or stimulants
- If you are struggling to cope
- If you are self-harming
- If you think about suicide
- If you experience the signs outlined on pages xvii–xviii.

It is good to take charge of your well-being and take steps to manage stress, but it is also good to seek out professional information, advice, guidance or support. It is better to seek help too early than too late!

1

Appreciate 'helpful stress'

Understand its benefits

How can this help?

Short spells of stress are useful. Those who excel at exams, sports, performance or in business make use of the sharpened focus and increased energy that accompany stress. Stress can help students to achieve better. Research suggests that embracing stress is associated with better health and productivity.[5] Remembering that stress has beneficial effects, and isn't necessarily something to fear, can help dispel some of its perceived threat.

Considering your responses

If your responses to the questions above indicate that you hadn't really thought about how stress might be beneficial, then an important first step is to appreciate that stress isn't necessarily a bad thing and can actually be turned to good use.

 Do I ...?

1. Do I tend to regard all stress as bad?

   Yes   **No**

2. Do I tend to fear stress in case I lose all control or everything collapses?

   Yes   **No**

3. Do I tend to avoid anything that might be stressful for me?

   Yes   **No**

4. Do I appreciate the advantages of feeling some stress if managed well?

   Yes   **No**

 See also

Ways 2, 3, 4, 5, 6

 To do. I will ...

Recognise how stress can help

If you feel stressed, bring to mind how it can be an asset. Energy levels, concentration and problem-solving are affected negatively by too much stress but, conversely, benefit from short-term acute stress.

Short spells of stress can energise us and develop inner strength. This is especially so when we can tune into points of interest or excitement.

The important thing is to harness early signs of stress to stimulate you into action and reduce last minute panic and protracted anxiety.

Ways stress can help

Below are some ways that stress can be helpful. **Highlight** any of value to you.

To feel charged and energised
The adrenaline that accompanies it is like an electric charge, encouraging the body to move and take action. We can use that!

As motivation to get things done
Use it as a spur to start early on study tasks. Planning, organisation and early starts reduce study-related stress later.

To boost academic abilities
In short spells, stress can raise mental alertness.
This can be directed to study tasks.

To improve memory
and recall, for study, exams, interviews, jobs and everyday life.

To combat tiredness
Adrenaline helps us fight fatigue and pain, increasing endurance. It helps us to keep going when we have a deadline to meet.

2

Harness the benefits of stress

Make helpful stress work for you

Do I ...?

1. Do I use the energy that comes from stress to achieve more?

   Yes   No

2. Do I know how to make stress work for me?

   Yes   No

3. Do I miss out on opportunities or under-achieve because I avoid stress?

   Yes   No

4. Am I open to working with stress so that I feel more in charge of it?

   Yes   No

How can this help?

We can all learn to make stress work for us – and that is especially important for students. Learning to use stress helps us to reduce its negative power whilst enhancing our performance, energy and strength. Doing this properly is important, so that stress is experienced for short spells rather than all the time.

Considering your responses

If your responses to the questions above indicate that you could benefit from harnessing the energies and abilities that are enhanced by stress, but are not sure how to do so, then the suggestions opposite provide a starting place. The most important thing is to understand that we can manage the levels of stress we experience, such as through the way we exercise our minds and body. We can make stress work for us.

See also

Ways 1, 3, 4, 5, 6

To do. I will ...

Use stress as an asset

Below are some actions you can take to harness stress. Select ✔ those you consider would be useful and manageable for you.

- [ ] Embrace stress as a potentially helpful aspect of life.

- [ ] Recognise your body's stress response as a helpful sign of energy you can use.

- [ ] Recognise the 'fight, flight or freeze' response and decide to 'fight'.

- [ ] Recognise that stress shows you care – use that as motivation.

- [ ] Recognise that taking on stressful situations can make you stronger and better at coping with future challenges.

- [ ] Give yourself a 'pep' talk to motivate yourself.

- [ ] Remind yourself of how you have already grown through adversity.

- [ ] Decide to feel excited about, and to welcome, challenge.

- [ ] List the skills or benefits you can gain from each challenge.

- [ ] Regard yourself as someone who can cope and learn from the stressful situation.

- [ ] Recognise stress affects everyone, and isn't 'proof of failure'.

- [ ] Take care of yourself, so you are better able to use stress.

3

Know the signs of excess stress

Get better informed

How can this help?

If we deal with high pressure often, we learn that we can cope reasonably well even with highly stressful times and events. Whilst that is good, it can mean that we don't notice when stress levels remain high or when we are starting to cope less effectively. Continued high levels of stress can be damaging. Catching the signs early helps you manage stress before it becomes too uncomfortable.

Considering your responses

If you are unsure about the signs of stress, consider the list on pages 8–9. Not everyone recognises when their stress is spilling over into distress. Consider whether you are taking signs of stress seriously enough. If you are uncertain, speak to a friend or family member who knows you well, or talk to a student counsellor.[31,32]

 Do I ...?

1. Do I keep generally well-informed about stress and its risks?

   Yes ☐ **No** ☐

2. Do I know the signs generally associated with excess stress?

   Yes ☐ **No** ☐

3. Do I know my own signs for being over-stressed?

   Yes ☐ **No** ☐

4. Do I generally spot signs of stress in myself early, so I can deal with them?

   Yes ☐ **No** ☐

 See also

Ways 1, 2, 4, 5

 To do. I will ...

Know what to look out for

Be aware of the feelings, thoughts, behaviours and physical symptoms associated with excess stress.

Identify your own signs of stress

Everyone is over-stressed at some time. Consider how this manifests in you: see the self-assessment on pages 8–9.

Recognise the signs

Look for connections

Stress symptoms are interconnected. For example, worry can lead to lack of sleep or poor eating patterns; lack of good sleep or poor nutrition can make worries seem worse. This can feel as if you are caught in a vicious cycle.

Look for clusters

It is unlikely that anyone experiences every symptom associated with stress: you could be over-stressed even if you don't experience many of those listed on pages 8–9. Look for a cluster of symptoms and consider how these affect you.

Be aware of others' stress responses

Not everyone experiences or expresses stress in the same way. Consider the signs in people around you.

Recognise the signs

Consider these typical signs of stress. **Highlight** any you recognise in yourself. Select any that are similar to what you are experiencing.

Feelings

- Frequent feelings of anxiety
- A sense of dread or panic
- Lack of interest in anything
- Impatience and frustration
- Can't switch off from worries
- Feeling isolated, lonely or alone

- Feeling you want to hurt yourself or someone else
- Feeling depressed
- Feeling overwhelmed/burdened
- Losing your sense of humour
- Concerned about your health.

Ways of behaving

- Can't relax or enjoy anything
- Tearfulness or crying easily
- Lose temper/get irritated easily
- Snapping or swearing at others
- Aggressive behaviour/language
- Increased drinking or smoking

- Eating too much or too little
- Nail biting or picking at skin
- Self-harming, or considering this
- Hard to concentrate/stay on task
- Difficulties making decisions
- Denying anything is wrong.

Physical signs

- Headaches/migraines
- Difficulties with sleeping
- Getting ill often
- Shallow or rapid breathing
- Tired all the time
- Indigestion, heartburn

- Grinding teeth or clenching jaw
- High blood pressure
- Chest pains
- Loss of interest in fun/pleasure
- Feeling sick, dizzy or faint
- Panic attacks.

Patterns of thoughts

- I have just too much to do
- These thoughts keep going round and round in my head …
- My head feels like it's bursting
- I feel like I can't breathe!
- I'm scared, I'll cry – I mustn't
- It's other people – winding me up

- They expect too much of me
- It's all getting out of control
- I can't handle all this pressure
- I can't bear the uncertainty
- I am such a failure!
- I can't let anyone know …
- I just want to give up!

What to do next

Be honest and realistic about the level of seriousness – a few mild signs occasionally? Or frequent feelings that you can't cope? Are you or others at risk? Would it be sensible to talk things through?

- If you can self-manage your stress levels, be active in doing so.
- Take steps to maintain general stress at a reasonable level.
- Use high stress for short spells of time only.

Rarely over-stressed?	Use good stress management habits to keep things that way.
Symptoms quite mild or infrequent?	Exercise self-help if you feel the signs are at a manageable level.
Getting too stressed?	Take steps now to reduce stress.
Quite stressed a lot of the time?	Make an agreement with yourself to form new stress-management habits. Select those 'Ways' that suit you. It usually takes 2–8 weeks' practice to shape a new habit.
Highly stressed?	Seek support. See page xxiii.

4 Recognise your own stress triggers

Become more self-aware

How can this help?

Because everyone is different, there isn't one set of triggers associated with excessive levels of stress.[3,15] This makes it important to be self-aware, so we know the kinds of circumstances in which we are personally most sensitive to becoming over-stressed. We can then take better care of ourselves at such times and take steps to manage our stress level better.

Considering your responses

If you don't know or are unsure, consider these typical triggers:

Big life changes. Uncertainty. **Bereavement.** Illness. **Financial worries.** Moving home. **Being tired.** Poor nutrition or feeling hungry. **Road rage.** Self-doubt. **Being bullied.** Important deadlines. **Exams.** Health concerns. **Difficulties with relationships, friends or family.** Comments on social media. **A particular sound, place, comment, demand, time of day, or thing people say or do.** Competing demands on your time.

 See also Ways 2, 3, 5, 6

 Do I ...?

1. Do I know which aspects of study make me feel most stressed or anxious?

   Yes **No**

2. Do I know which aspects of student life are the most stressful for me?

   Yes **No**

3. Do other things get me stressed and anxious frequently?

   Yes **No**

4. Do I know when I am likely to feel more stressed than at other times?

   Yes **No**

 To do. I will ...

Increase your awareness
of your personal stress triggers …

Pause and take note
When you notice you are feeling highly-stressed, pause and consider what is going on for you now that could be contributing to this.

Ask a friend
Ask someone who knows you if they have noticed that you get stressed at particular times.

Consider past stress
Think about times in the past when life seemed difficult or you found it harder to cope. What kinds of things were going on? What happened just before you felt most stressed?

Keep a record
Jot down those things that are going on, or went on in the past, around the times you felt most stressed. Make a list.

Look for patterns
Check what kinds of things come up more than once on your list. Look for things that seem to occur in combination, too.

5

Take signs of stress seriously

Take action to protect yourself against excess stress

How can this help?

Don't just dismiss physical signs of stress such as frequent headaches, migraines, tense muscles and jaw, or grinding teeth at night. Look at the pressures that could be giving rise to these. Not dealing with excess stress can make the symptoms worse, leading to further problems. It is important not to let current stress create more anxiety and stress later.

Considering your responses

Give thought to whether your responses suggest you need to give more attention to causes of stress, or whether you need to keep short-term causes of stress in perspective so that they don't distress you more than they need to. Either way, take yourself seriously. Take steps to ease the stress you are feeling now and to guard against excess stress in future.

 Find out more

See www.mentalhealth.org.uk

 See also Ways 3, 4, 6, 16, 39

 Do I …?

1. Do I monitor for signs of stress?

   Yes   No

2. Do I take these signs seriously?

   Yes   No

3. Do I tend to ignore my stress?

   Yes   No

4. Do I watch out for my stress triggers and take steps to manage these?

   Yes   No

5. Do I worry too much about stress that is likely to be short-lived?

   Yes   No

To do. I will …

Take practical steps

Understand the connections
Look for connections between how you are feeling and what is going on in your life. Consider both the potential causes and effects of the stress – sometimes these are similar. For example, lack of sleep can cause stress and result from stress. Focus on causes first.

Recognise the 'self-sorters'
Identify which of the underlying causes of your stress will go away eventually anyway – such as an exam or difficult essay.
Remind yourself these won't last forever.

Re-evaluate your lifestyle
Are you attending enough to your basic human needs: sleep, nutrition, water, exercise, rest and relaxation? Are you trying to do too much in too short a time? Are you taking good care of yourself? Do you need to form some new habits to better protect you against excess stress (see pages x and 104–5).

Prioritise practical steps
Make a list of the things causing you stress that you can do something about. **Highlight** the things you can do that will have the most impact or make you feel better now. Choose just one or two to get started. Doing something makes you feel better than doing nothing at all.

6

Take charge!

Gain control

How can this help?

Taking charge is important because, when we are stressed, it can feel as if everything is getting out of our control. It isn't. There is always something that can reduce the problems or the way we are experiencing them. Doing nothing just adds further to our stress. The moment you decide to take action to sort things out, you start to take power into your own hands. That is important to finding a workable solution.

Considering your responses

If your responses suggest you are under more pressure than you feel you can cope with, then it is important to take action. Just talking and asking for help is a good start. The earlier you begin, the sooner you can ease the stress. For the longer term, devise a strategy that helps you to build your capacity to cope and to maintain stress at manageable levels.

 See also Ways 1, 2, 3, 5, 8, 16

(?) Do I …?

1. Do I feel I am under more pressure than is good for me?

   Yes　**No**

2. Do I think I can cope well with stress?

   Yes　**No**

3. Do I have a plan for dealing with things that are causing me stress?

   Yes　**No**

4. Do I have a strategy for helping me cope with high stress situations?

   Yes　**No**

To do. I will …

Devise a personal strategy that works

Find the cause(s)

Pause to think through what is causing you to feel stressed now. It might be one of your stress triggers (Way 4) or something in your immediate circumstances, or many things accumulating and taking you to your 'tipping point' for stress.

List your options

Write these down and think about the pros and cons. Investigate the possibilities. Ask the experts at uni/college. Give yourself choices.

Focus on what you can do ...

don't dwell on the things you can't do anything about just now.

Make decisions

When you know your options, decide on your way forward. Making decisions relieves stress. Get good advice so that you make wise decisions.

Create a resilience toolbox

Try out some of the 50 Ways to find the best stress outlets for you and to develop coping strategies.

Get a second opinion

When we are stressed, it is harder to see ways forward. It is useful to get help from someone who can give an independent perspective and help you clarify your options.

Avoid unhealthy tactics

It can be tempting to turn to alcohol, smoking, drugs or self-harming behaviours of various kinds. These are 'false friends' when stressed, and usually add to problems you'll need to deal with.

7

Get physical!

Feel good through more movement

How can this help?

When we feel stressed, we are less likely to exercise.[33] Research shows students who exercise 20 minutes three times a week are less likely to report mental health concerns. Physical activity that increases the heartrate triggers release of BDNF; this acts as a 're-set' mechanism so that we feel clearer, refreshed and happier after exercise. We can also feel more relaxed and happier from the endorphins released during exercise, and from using up excess energy and adrenaline. Exercising with other students is especially good for stress.[29]

Considering your responses

If your responses suggest you are moving about too little in the day, consider how you could build the number of minutes each day that you are doing exercise, moving, or just standing! There are many ways to build exercise into your day on a student budget. See some opposite.

 See also Ways 14, 24, 29, 49

 Do I ...?

1. Do I get exercise for at least 20 minutes three times a week?

   Yes ☐ **No** ☐

2. Do I build physical activity into my daily routine?

   Yes ☐ **No** ☐

3. If I am feeling stressed, do I tend to stay in, missing out on social exercise?

   Yes ☐ **No** ☐

4. If I am feeling anxious, do I make a point of doing some strenuous exercise?

   Yes ☐ **No** ☐

 To do. I will ...

Devise a personal menu of physical activity

Join a student sport team
Exercise whilst making friends, being part of a team, and getting advice from coaches.

Dance
Put on music that makes you want to dance around your room. Go out dancing. Join a dance class.

Join the campus gym
There are usually reduced rates for students.

Use a Personal Trainer App
There are lots to try out – such as Nike+ Training Club or MyFitnessPal.

Clean your room!
You gain exercise and the room feels much nicer to be in afterwards!

Green fingers physical
Join a 'Green fingers' or environmental group on campus or in the local community.

Exercise at your desk
Try out stretches you can do without leaving your desk![34]

Go for a wander
Give yourself a break. Cycle, run or walk around the area.

Use online resources
Check out the huge range of keep-fit, exercise, yoga and dance videos free on YouTube.

Walk or run every day
Cheap and easy. Great for some thinking time alone. Or form a group (or join one) at your level.

8

Talk it through!

Share your problems with people who care

How can this help?

Managing stress often involves some consideration of areas that are painful for us, whether that is a bereavement, the end of a relationship, or doubting our ability to cope. Speaking about such things can be painful too, but many people find that they do feel much better after talking about their concerns. This is why so many therapies are based on talk. It helps you feel less alone with whatever is troubling you. It can also help clarify the issues and ways forward.

Considering your responses

Consider whether you are bottling things up and, if so, whether it might be a relief to talk. You can choose what details to disclose or keep private, and you can end a conversation when you have said enough. Think about what you would feel safe to confide initially and to whom.

To do. I will …

Do I …?

1. Do I keep my problems to myself?

   Yes **No**

2. Do I find it difficult to talk to others about my own problems?

   Yes **No**

3. Do I worry about talking to a professional in case other people find out?

   Yes **No**

4. Do I try to spare other people from knowing how bad I feel at times?

   Yes **No**

5. Do I try to keep my stress a secret?

   Yes **No**

Find out more

For useful resources, see pages 110–13

See also

Ways 5, 6, 27, 45, 46

It is good to talk!

Don't bottle things up
Be open to talking about what is going on for you.

Find the right person
– someone who puts you at ease, cares about you, or is trained to listen.

Talk to a friend
Don't talk about problems all the time but do share what concerns you with a good friend or two.

Talk to family / partners
It is natural to want to spare those close to us if we feel stressed but they can probably tell anyway. Let them help. Strong relationships help reduce stress.

Talk to a professional
A chat at an early stage with someone who is trained to listen can help to clarify your thoughts and find a way forward.

Share in a group
It can really help to hear what other people are going through. Whether or not their experiences are the same, there will be similarities.

Listen to suggestions
When stressed, it is easy to dismiss even useful ideas. Pause and consider whether some aspect of a suggestion might help.

9

Get enough (good) sleep

Give your mind and body time to replenish

How can this help?

Student lifestyles, with many late nights, disrupt natural sleep rhythms. Around 70% of students don't get enough sleep, with half reporting daytime tiredness or low energy. More than 4 out of 5 say sleep affects their performance.[35] Good sleep improves memory, performance, mood, and grades. Missed sleep, on the other hand, is associated with poor attention, recall and reasoning, as well as lower grades, stress, depression, paranoia, and even an increased risk of accidents. Stress affects sleep, and lack of sleep adds to stress.

Considering your responses

If your responses suggest you are not getting enough sleep, consider the range of potential negative effects of that – and take these seriously. If you are feeling low, consider how much good sleep you have had lately. Take steps to get more of the sleep that nourishes and refreshes you.

 To do. I will …

 Do I …?

1. Do I get 7–8 hours' sleep a night?

   Yes **No**

2. Do I feel tired during the day?

   Yes **No**

3. Does stress affect my sleep?

   Yes **No**

4. Do I prepare well for sleep?

   Yes **No**

5. Do I 'pull a lot of all-nighters'?

   Yes **No**

 Find out more

For more about sleep in student life, see Hershner et al. (2014)[35]

 See also

Ways 13, 16, 21, 48, 49

Be sleep wise

z z Z

Power down before sleep
Don't go to bed with a racing or agitated mind. In the hour before bed, avoid technology and games altogether: keep these and phones away from where you sleep!

Ease into sleep
Listen to relaxing music, take a warm bath, read, meditate, make a milky drink.

Watch caffeine intake
Avoid caffeine, energy drinks and other stimulants after midday.

Use a regular sleep routine
Get your brain and body used to the expectation of sleep at a certain time. Follow a routine in preparing for sleep. Go to bed at the same time as often as you can.

Don't lie awake worrying
Get up for a few minutes. Walk around and stretch gently. Use relaxation techniques to calm your mind before going back to bed.

Avoid 'All-nighters'
Research shows it can take several days to restore your performance after missing a night's sleep – not good for exams!

Catch up on missed sleep
If you miss sleep at night, make time for a 20–45 minute 'power nap' in the day or early evening. Sleep in, or take naps to catch up on sleep during the week.

z z Z

10 Combat homesickness

Give yourself time to settle in!

How can this help?

The student helpline, Nightline, found that around a third of students experience homesickness at some time (2013).[36] It can be tiring, disorientating and unsettling to adapt to new places and people, especially when you miss home, friends and all that is familiar to you. It is important to allow yourself time to build new social networks and to let your new surroundings feel like a second home.

Considering your responses

If your responses suggest that homesickness is getting in the way of your studies or making you unhappy, don't suffer alone and in silence. Don't rush home either. Be kind to yourself whilst sticking it out. You will feel more 'at home' if you become familiar with the campus, use its facilities, join in and get to know a few more people.

Do I ...?

1. Do I feel homesick?
   Yes **No**

2. Am I spending too much time on my own?
   Yes **No**

3. Am I withdrawing from classes and/or from student social life?
   Yes **No**

4. Am I thinking of giving up my course because of homesickness?
   Yes **No**

Find out more

Nightline (2013)[36]
www.nightline.ac.uk
See page 116.

See also

Ways 20, 24, 39, 42, 48

To do. I will ...

Make a home away from home

Acknowledge your feelings
It is natural to feel homesick. Don't push away the feelings but don't give in to them either: notice them and feel appreciation for people and things you miss.

Take time to adjust
It takes a while for new surroundings to become familiar. Let it happen.

Bring a touch of home
Bring a few favourite items that remind you of home in a good way – including music and recipes.

Get immersed in student life
Get out of your room, meet people, take up new things. Stay occupied with things you enjoy. Don't give yourself time to dwell on what you might miss.

Keep in touch
Phone home or Skype regularly but not constantly. Don't go home in the first weeks – settle in first and plan a trip home you can look forward to!

Share experiences
Others will miss home too. Share photographs and stories of home. Cook each other favourite meals.

11

Laugh more!

Find the funny side

How can this help?

A good laugh, or even anticipating one, creates positive physical responses.[37] Laughter charges and cools your stress response so you feel good and more relaxed. It can increase oxygen intake, endorphins, blood circulation and muscle relaxation, all of which reduce symptoms of stress. It reduces levels of the potentially harmful stress hormone, cortisol. Studies have associated laughter with other benefits. Just 10–15 minutes of laughter a day can burn off 40 calories. A good sense of humour reduces the likelihood of heart disease.[38]

Considering your responses

Consider whether your responses suggest you could do with more laughter in your life. If so, look for opportunities to find ways of exercising and developing your sense of humour. Aim for kind humour – anger and hostility can be funny but tend to feed stress rather than reduce it.

 See also Ways 20, 32, 36, 43, 50

 Do I ...?

1. Do I laugh enough?
   Yes ☐ **No** ☐

2. Do I laugh a few times every day?
   Yes ☐ **No** ☐

3. Do I find humorous aspects to annoying everyday situations that affect me?
   Yes ☐ **No** ☐

4. Do I look for opportunities to enjoy a good laugh?
   Yes ☐ **No** ☐

5. Am I losing my ability to laugh?
   Yes ☐ **No** ☐

 To do. I will ...

Find out what makes you laugh and add it to your daily routine

Gather comic books
Have texts and images to hand that make you laugh when you browse them.

Watch YouTube videos
Browse the most popular humorous YouTube videos. Make a long list of your favourites so that you have plenty to choose from when you need a laugh.

Take yourself less seriously
Pause to consider your situation and find the humour in it. Many comedians form their routines from events that were difficult, painful or embarrassing to them. Finding the humour doesn't mean the serious aspects cease to be important.

Humour in exaggeration
Write down your day, exaggerating wildly about small things that are annoyances or setbacks but not really that bad in themselves. Read it through as if you were a TV or radio comic: find the humour in it.

Use radio and TV
Find programmes that make you laugh. Download or store them to share, ease stress, wind down before sleep or just to enjoy them.

12

Get well organised

Take control of space, time and tasks

How can this help?

Studies suggest that our brains are constantly scanning their surroundings and looking for signals that suggest we need to expend energy. It registers mess and disorganisation as an energy demand, which can feel stressful. In addition, being untidy or disorganised usually results in wasted time, unfinished tasks, missed appointments and a sense of things being out of control.

Considering your responses

If your responses suggest that gaps in time-management, planning and organisation are adding to your stress levels, or just make you less effective, then addressing this can reap a wide range of benefits.[39,40] Even a little more clarity about what you are doing and where to look for things can reduce mental clutter and ease your day.

 Do I ...?

1. Do I waste time looking for keys, folders, files, wondering where I put things?

   Yes   **No**

2. Do I tend to be late or miss appointments?

   Yes   **No**

3. Do I feel time runs away from me?

   Yes   **No**

4. Do I worry about not getting assignments or other things done in time?

   Yes   **No**

 See also

Ways 18, 23, 28, 31, 38

 To do. I will ...

Organise, plan, simplify

Decide ✔ on actions you will take!

Simplify
Keep one 'To Do' list, one diary, one file per subject.

Set time limits
Don't use complex organisation as a time-wasting distraction. Put aside short spells every day to sort, organise, plan.

Declutter
A clear space calms and clears the mind. Create some clear surfaces. Tidy things away when you finish with them. Throw away stuff you don't need.

Manage losable items
Use a small bright bag you can't miss to hold all small items such as keys, memory sticks, lip balm, etc.

Organise key information
Write everything into your diary/planner – birthdays, tutor tips, lists, etc. so you don't need to clutter your brain with them![39]

Update your daily checklist
… and gain the satisfaction of crossing off completed items and staying on top of things.

Write yourself reminders
… on sticky labels to put into your planner.

Organise your notes
Sort these regularly. Date and label them so you can find material easily when needed.

13

Practise mindfulness

Enjoy the simplicity and calm that can arise from just being aware of your breath

How can this help?

Research by the University of Washington found that training in mindfulness along with 8 weeks of daily practice were more effective in reducing stress than relaxation techniques or using no technique at all. It also improved attention and memory.[41] Neuroscience has identified that the amygdala, the part of the brain responsible for stress and anxiety responses, is less active during meditation and in people who meditate. Images of meditators' brains indicate that brain areas associated with stress and anxiety are used less by them and even became smaller.[42]

Considering your responses

If you answered 'yes' to the questions above, then it is easy to get started and it doesn't need to cost anything. (NB if you have a history of mental ill-health, it is best to check with your doctor or therapist first and to join a class with an experienced teacher.)

 See also Ways 22, 25, 47, 48

 Do I ...?

1. Do I feel my mind gets too agitated?

   Yes ☐ **No** ☐

2. Do I need more calm in my life?

   Yes ☐ **No** ☐

3. Do I need a calming technique?

   Yes ☐ **No** ☐

4. Could I practise even for a few minutes daily?

   Yes ☐ **No** ☐

 Find out more

Cottrell, S. (2018). *Mindfulness for Students*[43] Also see page 116.

 To do. I will ...

Fit in some calming meditation

Sit upright in a comfortable position, eyes open or closed.
Commit to bringing your attention to your breath for a few minutes.

Notice the point where air enters your body.
Follow just one breath from start to finish. Then repeat.

When your attention wanders (it will!) just notice,
accept this, and bring attention back to the breath.

If your attention drifts to stressful thoughts or feelings,
again, just notice these, accept them, and bring your attention back to the breath.

Short term, this can be calming.
You have nothing to do at that moment except notice the breath.

With practice, focussing in on just a few breaths can be a quick,
easy way of calming yourself anywhere.

Longer term, this trains our minds to realise
that we are able to sit calmly with whatever comes up.[43]

Do it daily!

- A little every day is better than infrequent long sessions
- Start with just a few minutes
- Build the time up gradually
- 2–20 minutes a day works well.

Consider a group

- Ask others to join you
- Look for local groups.

14

Get outdoors into nature

Gain the benefits of the big outdoors

How can this help?

Being in nature makes us feel better. Hundreds of studies have found that being outside in nature, or just viewing it, is good for us physically, socially and mentally. It stimulates a great array of positive effects on our bodies, brains, nervous systems, emotions, feelings, thinking, creativity, health, generosity and our interactions with others. It even helps to build resilience and open us up to new experiences.

Considering your responses

Consider whether your responses are telling you that you could either get out into nature more, or absorb it more when outside. It is worth building some time in nature into your daily routine, to help reduce or avoid stress, but also to reap its wider benefits.

To do. I will …

Do I …?

1. Do I spend much time outdoors?

   Yes   No

2. When I am walking or running, do I take notice of the natural world I pass?

   Yes   No

3. Do I take breaks outdoors daily?

   Yes   No

4. When outdoors, do I absorb what is beautiful or pleasant around me, such as the colours, the clouds, the feel of the breeze?

   Yes   No

5. Do I appreciate nature enough?

   Yes   No

See also

Ways 15, 21, 24, 29, 32

Find the local beauty spots

Investigate the parks, ponds and areas with good views of trees and other plants. Find the roads with the best trees to look at. Take a short walk, or a longer one, there during a break or at the weekend.

Stand and stare

When outdoors, don't race through. Take a moment to pause and look. Notice what there is to see. Watch how the scene changes before you when the wind or the light alters.

Spend a few minutes in nature at least once a day

Feel it! Hear it! Smell it!

Let yourself experience the elements – the sun, wind, snow, even the rain! Notice how it feels on your skin. Take in the various scents. Listen to small sounds that you might not otherwise hear.

Join a group

Check out groups organised by your college or the local community for enjoying, or even clearing up, the local environment. It is a great way of contributing, as well as meeting people, building confidence and feeling better.

15 Watch nature on screen

... for less stress, more contentment

Do I ...?

1. Do I appreciate what I could gain from watching an amazing nature video?

   Yes **No**

2. Do I watch nature videos regularly?

   Yes **No**

3. Do I have images of nature in my room or on my device that I can see easily?

   Yes **No**

4. Do I pause and really take in images of nature?

   Yes **No**

How can this help?

The Real Happiness study (2017) by BBC Earth and Dacher Keltner from the University of California, Berkeley, reviewed 150 scientific studies and surveyed over 7000 people worldwide.[44] It found that watching nature documentaries, even in short clips, has an uplifting effect, improves health and mood, and reduces stress, anxiety and tiredness. It can generate feelings of real happiness, a sense of joy, contentment, awe, amazement, curiosity, and wonder! Still images can also help stress: looking at pictures of nature speeds recovery from acute stress.[45]

Considering your responses

If your responses suggest that you don't already watch nature documentaries, then these could provide great sources of wonder and well-being, without getting out of your chair! There is a lot of variety to choose from, so it's worth investigating the different options.

 See also

Ways 14, 32, 36, 48

 To do. I will ...

Sit back and enjoy
the wonders of the
natural world!

Watch *Planet Earth*

The powerful effects mentioned opposite were gathered from viewers watching the BBC's *Planet Earth* programme.

Build a bank of documentaries you enjoy

Dip into your favourites when you need an uplift.

Immerse yourself

Watch attentively, even if only for a few minutes. Really notice what is happening in the scene.

Take two minutes

If time is pressured, use great clips available online such as through Twitter and YouTube.

Share your favourites

– enjoy and discuss them with others.

Discover your tastes!

Night skies? Coast? Mountains? Animal documentaries? Or plants? Underwater? Deserts? Aerial views? Birds? Fish? Local or tropical? If one doesn't suit, there are many categories to explore.

It seems happiness comes from connecting to life, feeling part of a larger world and letting its beauty work on our minds and emotions.

16

Know your limits

Balance ambition and well-being

How can this help?

There is a delicate balance between high ambition and unrealistic goals. If you drive yourself hard to achieve success, or if you juggle many demands, it is all the more important to build your core strength. That includes building study stamina, health and general resilience – and being able to recognise when you are under too much strain. It is good to know how to reduce pressure for yourself – and also how to recognise what you can't resolve on your own at this time.

Considering your responses

Consider whether your responses suggest you have a good sense of what is realistic for you, and of when, why and how you push yourself beyond your limits. Some challenge is fine, but give thought to your limits and how you will recognise when you are approaching these.

 Do I ...?

1. Do I give myself strong messages about what I 'must' achieve or 'should be'?

   Yes ☐ No ☐

2. Do I think I must sort everything on my own?

   Yes ☐ No ☐

3. Do I feel I must say 'Yes' to every opportunity and request?

   Yes ☐ No ☐

4. Do I get stressed when I can't achieve all I set out to do?

   Yes ☐ No ☐

 See also

Ways 4, 13, 23, 32

 To do. I will ...

Set realistic goals ...

Decide ✔ which approaches below would benefit you.

Aspire – mindfully!
It is good to be ambitious, but do so with self-awareness. Consider well what is really manageable for you just now. Give success every chance, without holding too tightly to particular outcomes.

Be self-aware of impacts
Be alert to changes in your mood, emotions and behaviour.

Don't let goals rule
Use goals to provide direction and motivation. If they get oppressive rather than inspiring, set a more balanced set of targets.

Don't sacrifice self-care
If your health or sense of well-being starts to suffer, pause and rethink the demands you are making of yourself.

Seek an independent view
If you can't see a way of resolving difficulties, talk to a student adviser for an objective perspective.

It is OK to say 'No'
It is great to be open to new experiences and to be willing to help – but you have to say 'No' if you just can't take on any more!

Build endurance
If there are things that really can't be fixed, it is possible to learn to live with these. A combination of support, self-care and a positive attitude can help.

17

Start the day right!

How can this help?

A study by Rothbard and Wilks in 2011 found that the mood we have at the start of the day has a cascading effect on the rest of the day.[46] Starting in a negative mood leads to higher stress. A positive mood at the start of the day is associated with many benefits, such as more articulate speech, greater effectiveness at work and even better grammar, as well as reduced stress.

Consider your responses

Some people love mornings; others find it hard to drag themselves out of bed. If you find them difficult, you are nearer your stress threshold even before anything happens. If you find ways to manage that, then you can set up your whole day better.

 To do. I will …

 Do I …?

1. Do I get up at a different time every day?

   Yes   No

2. Do I tend to dread getting up?

   Yes   No

3. Do I find mornings are a chaotic rush?

   Yes   No

4. Do I usually leave home in a rush?

   Yes   No

5. Do I leave a lot of time yet somehow end up rushing?

   Yes   No

 See also

Ways 9, 18, 23

Take control of your day ...

Get up at the same time

This means you don't have to think about whether you want to get up – you just do it! It can help your body clock to settle, helping you to sleep through until your usual waking time.

Build a strong routine

Follow the same routine every day until eventually you start to complete it 'on automatic pilot'. It will be one less set of things to worry about. Your brain won't have to stress about what to do before it has woken up fully: it knows what to expect so can be calm.

Use a pleasing alarm

Use an alarm or wake-up call so you take control of when your day begins.

- Use a pleasant wake-up tone or music you like.

- Consider using an alarm that starts quietly and gets gradually louder, to avoid waking with a shocked jolt and adrenaline rush.

Leave 'just enough' time

- Each night, make a list of everything you have to do in the morning.

- Set the alarm to leave just sufficient time to get through your routine and list. In the morning, this helps to stay focussed. It avoids a sense of having plenty of time, then getting distracted and having a panicked rush.

18

Make time work for you

Find time for effective time management!

How can this help?

Students report that time pressures are a major source of stress. It is not surprising, then, that good time-management behaviours were found to be one of the most effective ways of reducing stress.[6,47] Effective time management is also associated with better academic performance, so good all round![48]

Considering your responses

When we are stressed, especially if that results from time pressures, it can feel as though there isn't time to pause and think about time. As a student, there is an unusual combination of independent study time, scheduled classes, rigid deadlines and new opportunities. This makes it all the more important to consider how you will use your time effectively.

 To do. I will …

 ? Do I …?

1. Do I feel pressurised by the number of things I have to get done?

   Yes ☐   No ☐

2. Do I plan out tasks so I know how much time I have, realistically, for each stage?

   Yes ☐   No ☐

3. Do I know where my time is used?

   Yes ☐   No ☐

4. Do I use effective time management skills?

   Yes ☐   No ☐

 Find out more

Cottrell, S. (2019). *50 Ways to Manage Time Effectively*[108]

 See also

Ways 12, 23, 26, 37

Take charge of time!

Prioritise

You can't do everything, so prioritise what is really essential and do those tasks first.

Know where your time goes

Be more aware of where you spend time currently. Monitor how long essential tasks take you so you can plan sufficient time to get these done without rushing.[40]

Watch for perfectionism

If you are time-pressured, be realistic about what is 'good enough'!

Get organised!

Good organisation and planning help you save time, whilst poor organisation wastes time unnecessarily.

Develop good diary skills

Make your diary your 'go-to' place for organising your time. Use a good student planner to sort and organise information, plan time short-term and long-term and keep track of time commitments. Check it frequently in the day, so you don't miss anything essential.[39]

19

Get social!

Build your sense of belonging

 Do I …?

1. Do I feel left out?
   Yes **No**

2. Does the campus feel alien?
   Yes **No**

3. Do I feel lonely or isolated?
   Yes **No**

4. Does it seem that everyone else fits in better than me?
   Yes **No**

5. Overall, do I feel I belong here?
   Yes **No**

How can this help?

The 2017 UPP report found 2 out of 5 students struggled with loneliness or isolation, especially early in the first year.[9] Such feelings can make students become withdrawn just when they need to be building social networks for friendship, study and contacts. Doing things with others helps combat excess stress. Even if it seems hard, it is important to get out and make opportunities to meet others. Student parties can be fun, but aren't the only or best way of getting to know others. If you aren't a party person, use other ways to meet people.

Considering your responses

If your responses suggest you feel outside of things, take steps to build your networks. Just passing smiles and greetings can make your day feel better. Remember that it takes time for other people to recognise new faces or to feel confident to say 'hello', too. You don't need to be an extrovert: lots of other people aren't either!

 To do. I will …

 See also Ways 10, 20, 24, 29, 42

Be around others ...

Study near others

Don't do all your study at home or in your room. Use the library and other social spaces on campus to create chances to spot familiar faces and meet others.

Attend welcome events

Get a sense of who is in your year and class. Smile and say 'hello' when you spot them around.

Be early to class

Great for feeling the place belongs to you, and for short chats.

Use queues!

Queues are great for striking up a conversation. Every connection adds to a sense of belonging, and could lead to other contacts later.

Don't rush away ...

Time just after class and events is perfect for suggesting going for a coffee, meal, event or exhibition with whomever is around.

Join in!

Let others become familiar with who you are. Take up a sport, join a club, join in conversations, take part in class discussions.

Don't expect too much!

You might make life-long friends in your first week. It is more likely that you will just meet people through whom you meet others who become your closest friends. Don't try to force friendships – just show interest, help others, and build connections.

20 Take stress out of meeting new people

Take it in steps

 Do I ...?

1. Do I enjoy meeting new people?

   Yes ☐ **No** ☐

2. Do I feel calm when meeting new people?

   Yes ☐ **No** ☐

3. Do I find it easy to put people at their ease when I first meet them?

   Yes ☐ **No** ☐

4. Do I avoid socialising because of anxiety about meeting new people?

   Yes ☐ **No** ☐

How can this help?

If you find social events taxing, take comfort in knowing you are not alone in this. Many people are nervous about what to say and find it hard to relax. Welcome events and parties can be especially demanding, especially if you are not fond of crowds and noise. If meeting people is stressful, take it in stages and don't expect too much from them. Aim to learn, at least, a few names and faces and to let others become familiar with seeing you around.

Considering your responses

If your responses suggest you struggle when you first meet others, don't let that put you off. It isn't necessary to make an amazing first impression – just explore a little and put a few basic blocks in place to build on if and when you meet again.

 See also

Ways 7, 10, 19, 21, 42

 To do. I will ...

Focus on other people not yourself

Decide ✔ on actions that could help you. Plan when to have a go!

Prepare in advance
You can feel more comfortable if you know more about people. Look at their social media sites – see if you have things in common. Check if others know them – find out what they are like.

Look pleased to see them!
People mirror unconsciously what they see in others. If you look pleased and excited to meet others, it is more likely that they will mirror that back.

Give a warm greeting
It just takes a smile and hello. Be prepared to be the first to speak.

Find out names
Ask for the name. Repeat it aloud – and then in your mind – to help remember it. Imagine it written on their forehead. You will feel more confident if you can recall their name next time you meet. If you forget, just ask.

Show interest in them
Focussing on others is a useful way of directing your attention away from your anxiety. It also makes others feel they matter, which helps them open up. Check that they have what they need – a drink, food, a seat?

'Ask' not 'tell'
Ask questions rather than talking about yourself or giving long involved responses. You don't need to invent imaginative questions – ask anything relevant to the person, time or situation.

Listen carefully
… so you can follow up with comments relevant to them.

21

Music to your ears!

Strike the right note!

How can this help?

Music and sound have been found to reduce stress – even stress associated with painful diseases and medical procedures.[49] Its soothing effects can be gained from just listening to it, or from singing, playing an instrument or writing a song. Self-selected music can have a significant calming effect – though rock music less so![50] Other sounds work too: rippling water can be even more soothing than music.[51]

Considering your responses

People tend to listen less to music when feeling stressed. Even if pressurised for time, it can be more productive to take time out to let music have its positive effects. Consider making time for varied music and sounds – some to release tension and relax, others to lift your spirits and improve your mood.

 To do. I will …

 Do I …?

1. Do I enjoy listening to music?

   Yes ☐ No ☐

2. Do I make space in my week to listen to music or soothing sounds?

   Yes ☐ No ☐

3. Do I listen to music that is uplifting and raises my mood?

   Yes ☐ No ☐

4. Do I listen to music that relaxes me?

   Yes ☐ No ☐

 See also

Ways 9, 14, 17, 32

Make time for music

Take in natural sounds

Before or after stressful events, relax by listening to wind in the trees, rippling water or waves on a beach. Sit for a while near a water feature on campus. Use recordings if you aren't near water.

Listen before sleep

Use calming music to power down before bed, to help you sleep.

Create your own stress-busting playlist

Stream or download music you find calming. Even if you don't usually listen to classical music, include some calming pieces for their good effects.

Sing along

Join in – sing, rap, shout. You don't need to be in tune to release the tension! Or go out with friends for a karaoke session.

Join a choir!

If you can hold a tune, join a choir! Enjoy that feel-good sensation whilst making new friends.

Listen to uplifting music

On your playlist, include music that raises your mood, such as music that makes you want to sing aloud or dance.

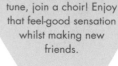

22

Park your troubles!

Give your mind a break from worrying

How can this help?

When we are anxious, it can seem as though time spent worrying is useful, even when our thoughts are unproductive and prevent us from finding solutions or falling asleep. It is easy to imagine that if we take our mind off the problem, even for a moment, we will never find a solution. Our brain puts survival first, so if we seem worried, it will happily join in and keep us on the alert for potential threat. It can be more useful to set times to give the brain a break and times to focus on issues of concern.

Considering your responses

If your responses suggest you can't switch off easily from your worries, then use strategies that send strong messages to your system that you will deal with your worries – but at the right time.

 To do. I will …

 Do I …?

1. Do I keep worrying about the same things over and over?

   Yes ☐ **No** ☐

2. Do I worry about things even when I mean to be doing other things?

   Yes ☐ **No** ☐

3. Do I keep going over things in my head even when trying to sleep?

   Yes ☐ **No** ☐

4. Do I feel anxious about letting go of things that are worrying me?

   Yes ☐ **No** ☐

 See also

Ways 9, 13, 18, 39

Create a space to leave your stresses

Write times for problem-solving into your diary
Help your system to relax, knowing you have set time aside to focus on matters that need resolving.

Create a 'parking space'
Create a mental 'parking space' to which you can send worries and tell them to wait. This could be your doorstep, a shelf, a box or bag – or anywhere you choose.

Send worries to the parking space
When anxieties intrude at unhelpful times, send them to the parking space. They will probably try to return. If so, keep sending them back to the parking space until you get used to leaving them there.

Temporary parking zone for all your worries

Reassure your worries
Talk to your worries. Tell them you will get to them at the right time.

Right place, right thought
Be firm with your thoughts if worries intrude. Repeat to yourself, so that your brain takes note that bed is for sleep, lectures are for listening, study time is for study, relaxation time for relaxing.

23 Create a realistic study schedule

Build a strong routine

 Do I ...?

1. Do I find it hard to settle into study?

   Yes ☐ **No** ☐

2. Do I put off study tasks a lot?

   Yes ☐ **No** ☐

3. Do I have a strong study routine in place?

   Yes ☐ **No** ☐

4. Do I get anxious about getting everything done?

   Yes ☐ **No** ☐

How can this help?

Many students find it hard to get down to study tasks, especially if they have to manage a lot of independent study time. It is easy to plan too much or too little study – and to delay or interrupt tasks continually, stop them early or get distracted during study. All this can affect grades and lead to unnecessary stress and anxiety. Drawing up a realistic study schedule clarifies what needs to be done and when. Sticking to the schedule provides a sense of accomplishment and reduces worry about whether you can get everything done.

Considering your responses

If your responses suggest that a good study schedule could help you, then the first task is to put time into your diary for drawing this up. It is useful to time yourself on key tasks – if you know how long these take you in practice, you can adjust your schedule if necessary, to keep it realistic. Once you have a schedule, the trick is to stick to it![39]

 To do. I will ...

 See also Ways 17, 18, 26, 31

Know when you will get stuff done!

Set enough time aside

... to complete essential tasks without excess pressure.

Check regularly

... several times a day, at the same times where feasible, so you can keep in mind what tasks are coming up later.

Keep it flexible

Allow yourself some planned rethinking of the schedule, so you can respond to opportunities that arise.

Keep it realistic

... so you don't need to be super-human to stick to it!

Use pencil

... so you can make changes if need be.

Build in regular short breaks

... to keep your brain refreshed and lively.

Put it where you can see it

... when you get up, and at any point in the day. If possible, keep it in your student diary/planner.

Study at the same times

Train your brain to expect to study at given times every day – less stress and good habit formation.

Build in some contingency

... so that you have time to spare if everything doesn't go to plan.

24 Change scene and break routine

Don't get stuck in a rut

How can this help?

A strong routine can be both useful and comforting (Way 23); changing our routine can also be helpful at times. Studies show that stress makes us more likely to stick to familiar habits even when we are aware they aren't really helping.[52] Sticking too closely to a routine can become dull and impair learning. If we keep seeing or doing the same things, it can seem as if there are few options. Making a change or altering a routine occasionally means we see and hear new things, which stimulates new ways of thinking, encourages creativity and helps with problem-solving.

Considering your responses

If your responses suggest that you are getting too fixed in your ways of thinking and doing things, consider what kinds of changes you could introduce to start to open up your world. It could be anything, from a change of address to varying your route to class.

 See also Ways 23, 32, 41, 50

 Do I ...?

1. Do I stick to habits that don't seem to be helping?

   Yes   **No**

2. Do I vary my routine deliberately to bring interest to my day?

   Yes   **No**

3. Do I feel 'stuck' in my life?

   Yes   **No**

 To do. I will ...

Try something new!

Rearrange the furniture
Give your room a fresh look!

Change of air!
Open the windows for a while – fresh air changes the ambiance!

Study somewhere new
If you always study in your room, study for part of the day at uni or in a social space. Vary your seat occasionally in the library.

Eat something different!
Invite a classmate to try out a café or restaurant. Or cook them a meal! Or cook one together.

Vary your route to class
Leave sufficient time to observe new things along the way.

Take up a new activity
Stimulate different brain cells and maybe get to meet new people too!

25

Relax with breathing exercises

Tools you can use anywhere

How can this help?

Breathing exercises can be used sitting, standing or lying down. They don't need to take long – a few minutes can make a difference and they don't cost anything! If you practise for a few minutes every day, you will have a useful tool to use when you need it – and also be more likely to remember to use it if need arises. That can add to your confidence to deal with stressful situations that arise.

Considering your responses

If you are anxious about using breathing exercises, speak to a health professional such as a GP or nurse for reassurance. If you are comfortable about learning these, have a go at the exercises opposite. Practise until you are comfortable using them in different situations.

 To do. I will ...

 Do I ...?

1. Do I feel comfortable about the idea of using breathing exercises?

   Yes ☐ **No** ☐

2. Do I remember to use breathing exercises to calm me down?

   Yes ☐ **No** ☐

3. Do I practise breathing exercises regularly?

   Yes ☐ **No** ☐

 Find out more

See www.nhs.uk/choices

 See also

Ways 13, 33, 47, 49

Breathe your way to calm

Don't force your breathing

If you start to feel dizzy or light headed, just pause for a while.

Find a comfortable position

… one that helps you relax.

Take 3 large slow breaths

… to stabilise your breathing.

Breathe deeper

Push your belly out as you breathe in. Fill your
lungs slowly, noticing your shoulders rise.

Like blowing bubbles …

Let your breath out slowly, as if blowing bubbles softly.

Focus on out-breaths

This helps slow your breathing and prevents hyperventilation. Count
to around 5 on the in-breath and 7 on the out-breath. If you are
anxious, it may take a few breaths to reach as high as 5 or 7.

3–5 minutes a day …

Become familiar with the exercises to gain confidence
using them if stressed or panicked.

Use mindfulness practice

Just observing your breathing can be relaxing.[43] See Way 13.

26 Develop good study skills and habits

Take charge of your academic success

 Do I ...?

1. Do I worry a lot about my grades?

   Yes ☐ **No** ☐

2. Do I lose sleep studying?

   Yes ☐ **No** ☐

3. Do I feel I don't need to improve study skills, because of my previous success?

   Yes ☐ **No** ☐

4. Do I feel unclear how to go about improving my grades?

   Yes ☐ **No** ☐

How can this help?

As might be expected, academic-related issues are usually the leading cause of student stress, especially anxieties about workload, grades and fear of failure.[9,53] High levels of stress are associated with weak academic performance.[54,55,56] As study challenges increase at every level, it is worth adapting and improving your study strategies to help you cope with these. Even students who do well academically can usually hone their skills and improve study habits further, for greater efficiency, effectiveness, calm and enjoyment.

Considering your responses

If your responses suggest that study-related worries are creating excess stress and affecting your well-being, then consider ways of sharpening your study skills to make learning more effective and enjoyable. A good strategy can mean more time for yourself, better grades and less stress.

 Find out more

See page 113 for books by Stella Cottrell on study skills, habits and strategies

 See also

Ways 12, 23, 31, 34, 37

 To do. I will ...

Devise a great study strategy

Investigate the requirements
Make sure you are clear of the syllabus and marking or grading criteria for your course each year.

Spot the difference
Check how requirements differ from previous years. If you are unsure, ask your tutors or the course director to clarify.

Effective and efficient
Look for ways of improving the quality of time spent in study, rather than studying long hours.

Share study tasks
Academic integrity is important so your work must be your own. That still leaves room for sharing study tasks such as searching for good sources of information, checking out new apps, or clarifying understanding of lecture material.

Use good materials
There is a huge variety of study skills resources to choose from. Use them to stimulate ideas about how to fine-tune your academic self-awareness, critical thinking skills, time management, academic writing, and test-taking strategies.

27

Write it out

Express, explore, clarify, resolve

How can this help?

Expressive writing can be therapeutic for many conditions such as negative moods, stress, anxiety and illness.[57,58,59] Writing things down serves a number of purposes, from knowing difficult things won't be forgotten, to allowing ideas to emerge about what would help. It can release the charge of pent-up emotion and can even boost exam results.[60] The most useful aspect is using writing to make sense of your experience.[61] Just writing basic thoughts and feelings about being at college/uni helps student health and stress.[62,63]

Considering your responses

If your responses suggest you are holding on to your worries, then it is worth seeing whether writing helps you to break that loop. A journal or notebook provides a different lodging place for your worries than your own head, as well as helping you to sort out your thoughts.

 See also Ways 4, 8, 39, 41, 44

 Do I ...?

1. Do I find it hard to talk about how I am feeling?

   Yes ☐ **No** ☐

2. Do I feel I am bottling things up that are causing me stress?

   Yes ☐ **No** ☐

3. Do I feel unhappy or anxious but am not sure why?

   Yes ☐ **No** ☐

4. Do the same worries preoccupy me?

   Yes ☐ **No** ☐

 To do. I will ...

Make sense of your experience

Keep it confidential
... rather than sharing whilst feeling stressed.

Keep it personal
... so you feel free to write what you want without worrying what others might think.

Choose your medium
... a journal, diary, notebook, file – or record yourself speaking.

Describe what happened
This reduces its power to hurt you, and can clarify your thoughts.

Write how you feel
... it can help you work out what it is you are really feeling.

Let it flow ...
Don't censor yourself or worry about style; just write what comes to mind until you feel like stopping.

Write to think
... to organise your thoughts and work out what is important to you.

Befriend your journal
... you can tell it anything! It won't judge you!

A daily help
Start with 5–10 minutes a day. Find a routine that works for you – every day, or once or twice a week.

28

Sort your finances

Ease financial stresses

How can this help?

Money matters are a major source of student stress. For many, managing finances is a new experience. It's easy to over-spend and it can be hard to find money for daily expenses. In the UK, over a third of students said financial worries affected their mental health; 69% female students and 55% males worried frequently about money.[64] There are similar findings from US studies.[65] Credit cards and 'payday loans' added to problems. Good money management might not resolve all financial concerns, but it can ease the difficulties and reduce the stress.[39]

Considering your responses

If your responses suggest that financial concerns are a cause of stress, then it can help if you know you are actively managing your money. If you feel uncomfortable discussing money worries, college/uni advice services are usually a great help, so it is worth giving them a go. They either offer relevant advice or can recommend good sources of help.

 See also Ways 12, 19, 30, 38

 Do I ...?

1. Do I worry a lot about money?

    Yes ☐ No ☐

2. Do I manage my money well?

    Yes ☐ No ☐

3. Do I avoid high interest loans?

    Yes ☐ No ☐

4. Do I feel I need good advice?

    Yes ☐ No ☐

 Find out more

UCAS www.ucas.com/finance/managing-money

Money Advice Service www.moneyadvice service.org.uk/en

 To do. I will …

Manage your money

Get good financial advice

Speak first to the relevant student support service at your university or college. Find out your options. Check which sources of advertised help you should avoid.

Avoid high interest loans

These add to financial problems. If you already have high interest loans, seek advice.

Beware of credit cards!

These can also add to problems.

Set a weekly budget

Put money aside for essentials. Divide the rest up between the weeks. Stick to your budget.

Monitor your money

Keep track of where you spend it. Check for unexpected areas of high spend on non-essentials.[39]

Buy or share?

Pause before buying, to check you really need and want it. Could you share the cost with someone else?

Learn cheap recipes

Learn to cook healthy cheap meals. Swap meals with friends.

Get bargains and discounts

When you need to buy things, use discount apps and websites, and places offering student discounts.

29

Take a walk!

Walk away stress; walk to prevent stress

Do I ...?

1. Do I look for opportunities to increase how much I walk during the day?

Yes **No**

2. Do I fit in a brisk walk on most days?

Yes **No**

3. Do I appreciate the benefits of a good walk?

Yes **No**

4. Do I walk rather than taking lifts and escalators or using the car or bus?

Yes **No**

How can this help?

A brisk daily walk of 20–30 minutes can boost self-esteem, calm the nerves and leave you feeling better for hours. When we walk, run or jog, soothing neurons are activated in the brain which, over time, can build our resistance to stress.[66] Walking is great because it is so easy, you can ask others to join you for a walk and it is a perfect way of getting out of your room for a change of scene.

Considering your responses

If your responses suggest that you don't get in as much walking as you could, then start to increase your daily walking quota. Use a variety of different walks. Enjoy improvements in your general fitness and stamina from building the amount you walk every day.

 See also

Ways 13, 14, 19, 24, 49

 To do. I will ...

Look for walking opportunities

Give it time

Build your walking speed and distance over at least 6 weeks. Notice and appreciate the feeling of your body in movement when walking!

Pause when studying

Take frequent breaks of a few minutes to walk around your room, library or campus.

Walk and talk

Chatting with a friend? Do it as you walk!

Count your steps

Count your footsteps as you walk – just start again if your mind drifts.

Social walk

Invite a friend to visit a park, walk into town, go shopping or walk to college together.

Get a walking buddy

… to help you keep a daily routine.

Enjoy nature

Go for a walk to see what nature has to offer today. Join a rambling club. (Way 14.)

Walk faster

Give your heart and lungs a work-out: feel happier and healthier.

Do a walking meditation

Walk for a few minutes just noting what is around you. Let your attention move to whatever comes up next, noting it without getting caught up in thinking or worrying about what you see.

30

Eat good mood food

Food affects mood – it's a chemical thing!

How can this help?

When stressed, we tend to turn to comfort foods, especially those rich in sugar or fats such as sweets, cakes, crisps, bagels and burgers that give a quick energy boost. Soon after, there is a big drop in blood sugar and hormone levels, draining energy and leaving us tired and susceptible to stressors. They also have a bad effect on health, fitness and general alertness.[67] Foods rich in omega 3 help to protect our neurons against stress.[68] Many other foods offer nutrients that contribute to health and help avoid stress.

Considering your responses

If your responses suggest that your eating patterns are reinforcing stress, then start to ease more good food into your week and gradually reduce junk foods and sugars. Just knowing the health implications of bad eating habits can make us feel stressed and drive us to our comfort foods. Break free of this by indulging in meals and snacks that are both healthy and good for stress busting!

 See also Ways 4, 5, 23, 49

 Do I ...?

1. Do I have stressful eating habits?

   Yes   **No**

2. Do I know which foods have a positive effect on mood?

   Yes   **No**

3. Do I eat much of these?

   Yes   **No**

4. Do I eat a lot of junk food?

   Yes   **No**

5. Do I consume a lot of sugar?

   Yes   **No**

 To do. I will ...

Eat yourself happy

Eggs
– for B vitamins and proteins.

Dark chocolate
Cocoa flavanols help mood and clear thinking, especially good for the kinds of intense thinking activities faced by students.

Pumpkin seeds
– for magnesium which helps avoid anxiety.

Dark leaves
– such as chard, kale, green cabbage – for many nutrients, including vitamins A, K, and potassium.

Foods rich in omega 3
– in fish such as salmon, sardines, canned tuna. Also in flaxseed and chia seeds if you don't eat fish.

Tea
Over time, drinking black or green tea reduces stress and boosts health.[69]

Chewing (sugar-free) gum
Studies show chewing flavoured gum for a few weeks improved mood, reduced cortisol, confusion, fatigue and stress. (It also increases blood flow to the brain, increasing alertness and improving performance on tasks that involve memory.)[70,71]

31

Devise a good exam strategy

Positive planning, calm preparation

How can this help?

Unsurprisingly, exams are a major source of anxiety for students. Lack of exercise around exam time and perceptions of having too much to learn contribute to high stress levels – for over 90% of students in some studies.[72] Fear of failure, poor time management and weak test-taking strategies are strongly associated with high exam stress.[53] To make matters worse, many students also neglect sleep, nutrition and socialising around exam time, too. A good exam strategy combined with sensible self-care help manage exam-related stress.[73]

Considering your responses

If your responses suggest that exam stress is a concern for you, then you are likely to benefit from using a long-term approach to develop exam-taking expertise and learn course material. Taking care of your well-being will help with both stress and exam performance.

 See also Ways 2, 9, 23, 37, 44

 Do I ...?

1. Do I get stressed about exams?

   Yes **No**

2. Do I plan towards exams in ways that reduce last-minute stress?

   Yes **No**

3. Do I build my exam-taking expertise to build my confidence and reduce stress?

   Yes **No**

 Find out more

See Cottrell, S. (2012). *The Exam Skills Handbook*[73]

 To do. I will ...

Prepare well for confident exam performance

Start your prep early

Don't leave revision until the last minute. Leave sufficient time to learn complex material early and revise it several times so it sticks.

Harness the stress

Use exam anxiety to spur you on to prepare well and to sharpen your focus. See Way 2.

Keep reviewing the material

Keep testing yourself on material until you feel you could answer questions in your sleep!

Draw up a good schedule

Plan carefully to cover a sufficient range of questions; plan when to retest your recall of material.

Make revision fun

Revise with others. Use fun quizzes. Devise memory joggers that make you laugh (or groan!).

Sleep, rest, relax

These help you absorb the material so don't sacrifice them. Beware of excess caffeine impairing sleep.

Use lots of dress rehearsal

Practise, practise, practise! Devise your own questions or use past exam papers. Answer these under conditions similar to a real exam.

Don't underestimate yourself

Trust that a good strategy is likely to get you through.

Keep exams in perspective

Don't over-estimate consequences of exam success or failure.

32

Manage your 'mind exposure'

Avoid the stuff of nightmares!

How can this help?

Whatever we see, hear and experience is food for the mind. Feeding our mind positive thoughts, humour and sensible interpretations of sensationalist stories, helps shape our responses to new situations. We can build resilience through exposure to stressful material. However, when we are stressed, we can be more sensitive to stories and images that feed our anxiety, depress us, scare us or raise our heartrate. That can affect our mood at the time and affect sleep later, reinforcing tiredness, anxiety and stress.

Considering your responses

If your responses suggest that you could be adding to your stress because of what you see and hear around you in the day or in the media, films, games or elsewhere, then give thought to what you are feeding your mind and why. If you need to see that material for your course, then consider when you access it, for how long and with whom.

 See also Ways 9, 11, 13, 40, 44

? Do I ...?

1. Do I spend a lot of time reading about other people's anxieties online?

   Yes ☐ No ☐

2. Do I think a lot about things that worry me when online or in the media?

   Yes ☐ No ☐

3. Do I expose my mind often to material that makes me feel scared or worried?

   Yes ☐ No ☐

To do. I will ...

Soothe your mind!

Avoid bedtime blues

Take especial care of what you expose your mind to in the hour before bed – things always seem worse once the light goes off!

Notice the connection

… become more aware of what kinds of material, games, sources of information (or people!) feed your anxiety. Cut back on these.

Beware the rumours

There are often sensationalist rumours circulating at college, uni or in workplaces. Few of these turn out to be true, or are not as bad as the stories going around.

Check the facts

If stories or articles are worrying you, check the details. The incidence of whatever is worrying you might be much less frequent than first reported and might not apply to your circumstances.

Select the right video games

Playing games can release stress but violent and aggressive games that trigger the 'fight or flight' response can leave you feeling 'wound up' or stressed and disturb your sleep.[74]

33

Relax jaw and fists

Smile, yawn, chew …

How can this help?

Stress can manifest as a tightening of the jaw, or of surrounding areas such as the temples, shoulders and neck. Many people hold tension in the jaw or hands, or clench their jaw or grind their teeth when under pressure. This can feed a cycle of pain, headaches, sleeplessness, stress and anxiety. You can relieve symptoms through massaging the area, exercises and general activity. A good laugh can help too (Way 11).

Considering your responses

If your responses suggest that you grind your teeth, clench your jaw or fists, or build up tension headaches, then consider these as potential signs of stress. Ideally, catch symptoms early and release stress before the pain settles in.

 Do I …?

1. Do I feel a lot of tenseness in my jaw?

   Yes   No

2. Do I grind my teeth?

   Yes   No

3. Do I tend to clench my fists?

   Yes   No

4. Do I get tension headaches?

   Yes   No

 See also

Ways 7, 11, 29, 35, 47

 To do. I will …

Release the tension!

Do 10 big yawns or smiles

Stretch the tension out of muscles attached to the jaw.

Side-to-side jaw exercise

Move the lower jaw quickly from side to side 20 times. Build to a speed you are comfortable with.

Massage the jaw

Using your fingertips, massage gently along the underside of your jaw from your chin to your ear. Repeat several times. Then pause at your ear and bring your fingers forward, feeling for the join of your jaw bone. Gently massage the join and surrounding area, moving your fingertips in small light circles. Extend these to take in your cheeks and the rest of your face. Use gentle pressure to avoid pain or bruising.

Unclench fists

Fists are used in aggressive situations: a clenched fist activates a stress response. If you find your hands clenched, just open them and relax your fingers.

Get a stress ball

Clenching and unclenching a stress ball or a similar item releases stress and relaxes your hands.

Other things?

Neck massages, acupuncture, acupressure and some yoga poses can also help.

34

Avoid task-switching stress

Remove a key source of stress

How can this help?

Although we often think we are great at multi-tasking, this is an illusion. The brain can only do one thing at a time (except for automated tasks such as breathing or walking). Every time we switch task, we work the brain harder and place it under more stress. Multi-tasking can trigger the flight or fight response, flooding us with stress chemicals that eventually leave us tired and stressed.[75] Studies show that splitting attention between tasks is linked to negative emotional responses to study.[76,77] Cutting down on task-switching or 'multi-tasking' eases a source of stress.

Considering your responses

If your responses suggest you switch tasks often, you have identified an important stressor (even if you call it 'multi-tasking'!). Research shows that those who think they are best at multi-tasking are least efficient at it, putting themselves under more stress.[78] Cut or reduce this stressor.

 Do I ...?

1. Do I multi-task a lot?

   Yes ☐ No ☐

2. Do I work with several pieces of technology open at once?

   Yes ☐ No ☐

3. Do I think I'm good at multi-tasking?

   Yes ☐ No ☐

4. Do I keep interrupting what I am doing to attend to something else?

   Yes ☐ No ☐

 To do. I will ...

 See also Ways 13, 17, 18, 40

Focus for efficiency

Focus on one thing at a time

Reduce the stress on the brain and body that comes from task-switching/multi-tasking.

Cross things off your 'To Do' list

Jot down all the things you need to do. Complete them in turn and cross them off your list. End the stress of having many tasks waiting for you to finish.

Use time blocks

Block time in your diary for specific tasks such as lectures, research, reading, writing, etc. – so that you can see the time is for just that ONE thing. Focus only on that task during that time block.

Set times for media checks

Rather than checking mail, texts, messages, tweets, etc. throughout the day, stressing your system, put aside specific times to focus just on those.

Do important things first

... create a more relaxing day by knowing these are now done.

35

Benefit from the power of touch

If it feels good, it does you good

How can this help?

Touch reduces stress hormones and boosts hormones such as oxytocin and serotonin that calm us and make us feel happier. Being in reassuring physical contact can have a calming effect. This can make a huge difference: in experiments, people were less anxious about receiving pain from electric shocks when holding their partner's hand.[79] We hold stress in our bodies and feel this in tight and painful muscles, stiff neck and shoulders, and general aches and pains. This can be soothed away by light touch or eased out through massage.

Considering your responses

Be open to receiving touch, either from family or friends if they offer. Alternatively, there is a wide range of different therapies and relaxing treatments that you can try as a treat. Or find a friend who is stressed and offer to exchange a shoulder massage. It works with pets too!

 See also Ways 33, 47, 50

? Do I ...?

1. Do I get hugs from friends?

   Yes   No

2. Do I hug my family enough?

   Yes   No

3. Do I go for relaxing massage?

   Yes   No

4. Do I like a pat on the back?

   Yes   No

5. Do I enjoy petting animals?

   Yes   No

 To do. I will ...

Relax those muscles

Ask for hugs

Ask your partner, family members or close friends if they would mind giving you a hug when you need one. If they are happy to do so, then don't be afraid to ask. Be open to giving them a hug when they need it too!

Pat on the back

If you are not keen on hugs and cuddles, a pat on the back also works and can feel reassuring. Ask a friend or family member just to put their hand on your back, or let them know you are happy to exchange back pats.

Treat yourself to a massage

Student Services may be able to recommend good local therapists; some offer student discounts. If you don't want a general massage, opt for a head or foot massage instead, or for a treatment such as shiatsu, aromatherapy, reflexology, or Touch For Health.

Learn how to massage

… a great way of learning to understand the power of touch and what works and doesn't work. You exchange massages whilst training and you gain a wonderful skill to offer to friends and family.

Pet an animal

If you like animals, then stroking cats, dogs and other animals is good for reducing stress. If you don't have a pet, there may be opportunities in the community to help with dog-walking or cat-sitting.

NB always respect other people's boundaries – and your own!

36 Trigger the 'happy' chemicals

Replace the habit of worrying

 Do I ...?

1. Do I feel a lot of guilt or shame?

   Yes   No

2. Do I worry a lot?

   Yes   No

3. Do I think about things I really enjoy?

   Yes   No

4. Do I spend enough time appreciating good things?

   Yes   No

How can this help?

Guilt, shame and pride use similar circuits in the brain. This means that when we keep worrying or feeling guilt or shame, our brain might actually be searching for a reward for worrying as if it had done this well. It interprets our worrying as something to be proud of. The way out of this is to reward it in other ways. When we focus our thinking on what we enjoy and appreciate, this boosts the release of the feel-good hormone, serotonin: the act of searching for positives helps your brain to let you feel good.[79]

Considering your responses

If your responses suggest that worrying is a habit, then it is time to form new habits that leave you feeling happier. These don't form overnight, but it can help to know we are creating them. Knowing more about how 'happy chemicals' work for us means we can take steps to generate more of them.[80]

 Find out more

Breuning, L. (2016).[80]
Habits of a Happy Brain

 To do. I will ...

 See also Ways 7, 19, 24, 35

Form the happiness habit!

Learn about the key 4

Our brain rewards us with 4 key sources of 'happy chemicals':

1
Dopamine, for the joy of discovery

2
Oxytocin, for bonding with others

3
Serotonin, for pride in being respected (or touched) by others

4
Endorphins, to help mask pain

Keep them flowing

The ideal is to establish habits that lead to a steady flow of these chemicals, rather than quick highs followed by sudden drops.

Win–Win

It involves doing things that can be both good for us and enjoyable: physical activity, socialising, and taking pride in our study and other achievements – all better for us than worrying.

List of 20+

Jot down at least 20 things you enjoy or appreciate about the world, life, study and learning (pages 108–9).

Look back at your list

… if in a low mood, to help balance your perspective.

Take pride in enjoyment

Pause to notice and absorb the moments you enjoy and appreciate them. Recognise the feeling of pleasure. Say thank you if relevant. Note it in your journal.

37 Reduce the pressure on assignment deadlines

Get ahead of the pressure points

? Do I ...?

1. Do I get anxious about meeting submission deadlines for assignments?

   Yes ☐ **No** ☐

2. Do I tend to put off work for assignments until the last minute?

   Yes ☐ **No** ☐

3. Do I often feel rushed to finish?

   Yes ☐ **No** ☐

4. Do I worry if several assignments have to be submitted at the same time?

   Yes ☐ **No** ☐

How can this help?

When assignment deadlines are drawing near, many students start to feel the pressure. Some leave assignments to the last minute in order to use the adrenaline rush to get them done. That can work, but not always. It can mean there isn't time to think things through well, and it is problematic if several assignment deadlines fall at around the same time. Starting earlier means you don't need to rush your work or worry so much about getting it done.[81]

Considering your responses

If you get worried or stressed about meeting assignment deadlines and don't like that last-minute rush, then you can take steps to reduce the pressure. Timing is key. Using 'First View' (see opposite) is a valuable initial step in bringing deadlines under your control.

 See also

Ways 18, 23, 26, 44

 To do. I will ...

Plan, Plan, Plan ...

Decide ✔ which actions could benefit you.

First View
Take an initial look at assignment requirements as soon as you receive them.
Know what to expect.

Remove the rush: start early
Begin as early as you can, even with just some initial thinking or reading. That
allows for more natural 'downtime' for the brain to work on issues, problems,
ideas.

Time it out
Work out how long the different tasks and components will take to complete.[40]

Plan for contingencies
Allow extra time – in case things don't all go to plan.

Schedule in detail
Map out exactly when you need to start each stage in a task. Stick to your
schedule. If you have to move a task, work out straight away when you will
do it.

Plan rather than panic
If submission dates cluster closely together, use good scheduling to manage
this. Start and complete an assignment early OR work on all in parallel, using a
detailed plan.

Take pride in planning
Give yourself credit for meeting set deadlines. Recognise the planning skills
involved: add them to your CV.

38

Make decisions

Know all your options

How can this help?

The act of making decisions, setting goals, choosing – these all trigger the brain to release dopamine. Boosting your dopamine levels makes you feel better. Making decisions has a calming effect generally, and reduces the pull towards negative impulses.[79,82] It removes some of the 'unknowns' so you know what to expect. That then puts you in a better place to plan how to put your decision into action and to get things done, establishing a virtuous circle.

Considering your responses

If your responses suggest that you find it difficult to understand your options or make decisions, then it is worth putting time into investigating the alternatives and taking steps that help you arrive at necessary decisions earlier rather than later. Poor decision-making can be a sign of stress so, if you feel stuck, ask for help in clarifying your thinking.

 See also Ways 6, 36, 37

1. Do I put off making decisions?

Yes **No**

2. Do I find it hard to make decisions?

Yes **No**

3. Do I feel I don't really have a choice in what happens?

Yes **No**

4. Do I feel anxious about making the wrong decisions?

Yes **No**

 To do. I will …

Remove the pressure of indecision

Investigate your options

Clarify what is, and what is not, possible. You might have more choices than you thought.

Write pros and cons

List points in favour of, and against, each choice. If still stuck, devise a rating system to find which option scores best.

Write down your choices

Draw them up so you can see them all clearly at a glance.

Decide on a direction

Set yourself a goal or target, so you have a focus for other decisions.

Decide 'good enough'

Consider what would constitute a 'good enough' outcome if you can't achieve your ideal.

Decide to look for positives

Not every decision will be a great one. Reflect on decisions you made in order to identify the best aspects and learn for the future.

Good enough assignment?

Decide how well you can complete each assignment, taking on board all your commitments and your well-being.

39

Accept your emotions

Acknowledge your feelings

How can this help?

Naming and accepting difficult feelings such as fear, anxiety and rage helps to prevent us from over-reacting and reduces negative emotions.[83] 'Accepting' means not judging emotions, pushing them away or pretending we don't have them. Research shows that accepting emotions doesn't block positive emotions nor make us feel worse. Over time, it increases well-being and helps us cope with stressful events such as sickness, bereavement and family crises.[84,85]

Considering your responses

If your responses suggest you are confused about what you are feeling, or constantly pushing away your emotions, or if you think a positive approach means maintaining an eternal smile, then give your emotions more consideration to help ease their effects.

 Do I …?

1. Do I pretend I'm not feeling difficult emotions such as rage, fear, anxiety?

   Yes   **No**

2. Do I push sad feelings away rather than just accepting that is how I feel?

   Yes   **No**

3. Do I feel I have to chase after positive feelings all the time?

   Yes   **No**

4. Do I feel I must keep a smile on my face?

   Yes   **No**

 See also

Ways 13, 27, 36, 45, 46

 To do. I will …

Be kind to emotions

Acknowledge your emotions

… accept they are there and a natural part of life.

Name your emotions

This defuses their power. Use 2–3 words, a simple metaphor or give them a numeric value. Searching for the right words or value activates the part of the brain responsible for thinking (the pre-frontal cortex), reducing activation of the part responsible for feeling emotions (the limbic system).

Let yourself feel

If you feel stress, anger, sadness, or other difficult emotions, accept that is what you are feeling now. It puts you in a position to manage the emotions rather than pretend they aren't there.

Recognise impermanence

Remind yourself that your feelings won't always be as intense and painful as they might be now.

Don't feed your emotions

Accepting emotions doesn't mean stirring them up to keep them alive. You can move on from them.

Change the situation

Accepting a feeling doesn't mean putting up with what caused it – especially if that involves bullying, or being badly treated.

40 Change your relationship with social media

Look less, enjoy more!

How can this help?

Social media adds to stress in many ways, from bullying or being shamed, to concerns about content or feelings of inadequacy about personal popularity.[86] 'Fear of missing out' drives high levels of anxiety.[87,88] For some people this involves checking social media every few minutes. Looking again at the way we use social media and changing our habits can ease stress and restore the enjoyment of using it.

Considering your responses

If your responses suggest that you are preoccupied by what others think and do via social media and/ or that social media add to your stress, then think again about your usage. You don't need to give up altogether if you don't want to, but you can change the way you use them so that they become useful and fun again.

 Do I …?

1. Do I worry about what I see or hear in social media?

   Yes ☐ **No** ☐

2. Do I worry about what is being said about me on social media?

   Yes ☐ **No** ☐

3. Do I worry about the number of followers, likes, etc. I get on social media?

   Yes ☐ **No** ☐

4. Do I worry about missing out if I don't keep checking social media?

   Yes ☐ **No** ☐

 See also

Ways 19, 41, 44, 46

 To do. I will …

Delight versus obsession?

Decide ✔ which actions you could take to benefit you.

When you use social media
Set yourself times for checking and enjoying social media – make a habit of not checking at other times. It isn't likely that you will miss out on much that would have a significant impact on your life.

What you use
Observe how much really useful information you pick up via social media and whose posts bring you enjoyment. Focus more on these. Cut out the dross. Look at how much time spent on social media is useful to you. Consider where you could save time for other things.

Why you use it
Bring greater awareness to why you are using social media. Consider whether it really fulfils those objectives or whether there might be better ways.

Take a reality check
Does the number of followers really matter? How many of them do you know well enough to care what they have to say? If there was something you really needed to know, would you find out about it anyway?

41 Express yourself creatively

Draw, paint, colour, cook ...

How can this help?

Research has associated happiness and greater feelings of satisfaction with being creative – just for the joy of it. By contrast, creating with a set goal such as a final product or meeting a deadline is associated more with stress. Creativity is associated with the totality of the experience of positive and negative emotions.[89,90] Any kind of creative expression, even colouring or cooking can absorb your interest, taking your focus off your worries and easing stress.[91]

Considering your responses

If your responses suggest you lack a creative outlet, consider what you enjoy or what interests you and start with that. It could be drawing, colouring, gardening, acting, designing a room, making a toy. Be open to just playing, experimenting, enjoying, messing up and trying again. Creativity works best if you do it for the love of it rather than to be perfect.

Do I ...?

1. Do I avoid creative expression because I think I am not 'artistic'?

   Yes   **No**

2. Do I inhibit myself creatively because of fears of what others might think?

   Yes   **No**

3. Do I have a way of expressing myself creatively?

   Yes   **No**

To do. I will ...

 See also Ways 11, 21, 27, 30, 50

Find your creative outlet!

Make time for creativity
Put time aside in the day so it doesn't get squeezed out.

Stimulate creativity
Use music, pictures, video, nature, art, history, science for inspiration.

Take a playful approach
Just see where your ideas or the material themselves lead you.

Don't be over-judgemental
If you produce something that looks truly dreadful, just laugh and have another go.

Enjoy the process
Find pleasure in just doing it.

Use all your senses
Take in the colours, shapes, tones, sounds, smells, and feel of things.

Don't over-think it
Let your unconscious have space to express itself through what you make. Don't be over-controlling.

Let the feelings out
Use the opportunity to express what is going on for you.

42 Help someone else

Make your day meaningful

? Do I ...?

1. Do I do much to help others?
   Yes ☐ **No** ☐

2. Do I feel I only have time for my own problems?
   Yes ☐ **No** ☐

3. Do I do anything really meaningful with my time?
   Yes ☐ **No** ☐

4. Do I think it would be rewarding to help someone else?
   Yes ☐ **No** ☐

How can this help?

When we are stressed, life can seem less meaningful. We can become over-focussed on our own needs, important though those are, at the expense of all else. It can help to think about others for a while and to do something we regard as worthwhile. A HEPI report on student mental health[21] recommended that all university students complete at least one volunteer placement – to improve their perception of their lives as worthwhile. Alternatively, you could offer to help on campus or just help out a friend.

Considering your responses

If your responses suggest you would benefit from focussing on someone else's needs for a while, then there are usually lots of opportunities. Some even provide a chance to travel, or take part in sports or the arts. If you are unsure, start by checking the opportunities available at your uni or college.

To do. I will ...

 See also Ways 10, 17, 20, 22, 24

Do something worthwhile

Decide ✔ actions you could take to benefit you and others.

Focus on someone else
Think what other people might need and how you could help.

Be a volunteer
Most universities, colleges and student unions offer a range of interesting options for volunteering. Check these out and see what is realistic for you.

Check local community and environment groups
There can be good opportunities – and you get to meet local people.

Support other students
Offer to train as a student mentor or buddy. Join a peer-assisted learning scheme.

Enhance student life
Offer to help your student guild or union. There are usually many jobs to be done – as officers, for student newsletters or radio, with surveys, welcoming new students, student health campaigns, etc.

Teach someone else
Teaching a concept to someone who is struggling helps not only them but also you. Feeling useful can alleviate stress and improve mood.

Learn first aid
You meet others, feel useful, are better placed to help others, and gain a useful life skill.

43 Befriend your mistakes

Find the learning opportunities

How can this help?

Being aware of mistakes and taking care to avoid errors are generally good behaviours – they help us to avoid all kinds of problems. If we worry too much about mistakes, they cease to be helpful. We are more likely to make mistakes when we are stressed so worrying about them can create a negative cycle.[92] As making mistakes really does help us learn, then we need to make some or we lose out. Some experts even advocate making deliberate small errors to help overcome excessive fear of mistakes.[93]

Considering your responses

If your responses suggest that you over-worry about your work not being good enough, the positive aspect is that you care about it. You might be putting too much focus on outcomes such as grades or good comments at the expense of learning from the process and gaining longer-term benefits.

 See also Ways 17, 23, 26, 44, 46

 Do I ...?

1. Do I feel a failure if I make mistakes?

   Yes   **No**

2. Do I feel like giving up when I don't get the grades I want?

   Yes   **No**

3. Do I avoid reading tutor feedback because I fear I got things wrong?

   Yes   **No**

4. Do I put off submitting my work because I'm anxious it isn't good enough?

   Yes   **No**

 To do. I will ...

Not brilliant – yet?

Can't do it – 'yet'?
Add 'yet' to your 'can't' statements. Learning is about finding a way.

Beware of perfectionism
Aim to do your best in the circumstances.
Beyond that, aim to learn from the overall experience.

Don't multiply mistakes
Don't let one mistake lead you to others. Don't delay submitting work –
that creates new problems!

Allow yourself mistakes
People tend to learn more from mistakes and failures
than from their successes. They provide a focus for improvement.

Welcome feedback
It provides useful insights on what is required or how to improve.

Treat 'criticism' as tips
Criticism pinpoints where others can envisage
a different way of doing things: that could be useful!

Look for solutions
If your work isn't as good as you would like,
identify what you get right already, and what to change.

Use an 'Action' list
Make a list of things to do differently next time.
Plan the details of how to carry this out.

44 Cultivate a balanced perspective

Avoid 'either/or' thinking

How can this help?

When we are stressed, it is easy to get locked into narrow thinking, noticing only what is wrong, or assuming that *either* a particular thing must be done or there is no other way. Manageable situations such as an unwanted change of room, tutor or study group can seem bigger problems than they are. Even poor grades or failed exams, though they might involve some rethinking or change, are not catastrophes and could create unforeseen opportunities. It can help to acknowledge that it could be stress that makes our options seem limited, and to seek out alternative views that show our situation in a different light. [94,95]

Considering your responses

If your responses suggest that you have a tendency to narrow your focus when stressed, you could benefit from pausing to put things into context. Taking in somebody else's point of view is a good starting place.

? Do I ...?

1. Do I get so caught up in situations that I can't find ways forward?

   Yes **No**

2. Do I often think, in the moment, that things are much worse than they are?

   Yes **No**

3. Do I worry about 'domino-effects'?

   Yes **No**

4. Do I tend to feel everything is ruined if some aspects don't go exactly to plan?

   Yes **No**

 See also

Ways 8, 24, 27

 To do. I will ...

Seek out alternative views

Get other opinions

Talk things through with someone who is likely to see things differently – not just those who will agree with you.

From someone else's shoes

What could be going on for those who annoy you? Would anyone envy your situation or view it differently?

Assume multiple solutions

Avoid thinking that there is only one way out. Jot down other potential solutions, even if it isn't immediately obvious how you might use these. Then work on these to find a way forward.

Describe without judging

Stand back and act as an observer. Jot down what is happening using just a few words or sentences, without judging others or defending yourself: We changed room; I have a new tutor, etc. Read it back and check how it sounds. Is it really worth your emotional energy?

Question worries critically

Check out your assumptions and whether things are as bad as they seem. Remind yourself of things you have achieved already.

45

Have a good cry!

Let it all out!

Do I …?

1. Do I let myself cry if I feel down?

   Yes　　**No**

2. Do I feel embarrassed if I cry?

   Yes　　**No**

3. Do I feel too numb to cry?

   Yes　　**No**

4. Do I feel I am allowed to cry?

   Yes　　**No**

How can this help?

Crying can have self-soothing effects, relieving pent-up emotions, easing sadness and grief, and improving mood.[96,97] This is more likely if you cry where you don't feel embarrassed, such as in private, watching a film or with someone you trust to comfort you. Crying releases toxins and the excess cortisol and manganese associated with stress; this lessens feelings of irritability, aggression, tiredness and distress. Tears contain other stress-related chemicals such as potassium and the hormone prolactin. Be aware: crying can make you feel worse at first, as the effects can take anything up to 90 minutes to kick in.

Considering your responses

If your responses suggest that you feel you aren't allowed to cry, or don't let yourself, then give yourself permission and recognise its value. If you are too numb to cry, it is a good idea to talk to a counsellor or equivalent to help you get in touch with your feelings.

To do. I will …

 See also Ways 9, 27, 39, 41

Move yourself to tears!

Don't fight it

We can tend to resist crying, as if to persuade
ourselves that things aren't really that bad,
or because we fear it suggests we can't cope,
or because it feels painful at first.
Then, when we do cry, it brings feelings of relief.

Recognise its value

Don't be embarrassed if you cry:
it is a survival mechanism,
boosts health and can ease your stress.

Write it down

Crying can clear your mind,
making it easier to write things down and work out a solution.

Drink water

Useful for easing stress and good
for rehydrating after crying.

Sleep it off

After a good cry, you can feel tired, dozy or relaxed –
a great time to catch up on missed sleep.

46 Accept yourself

Value more about yourself and others

Do I ...?

1. Do I worry I am not good enough?

   Yes ☐ No ☐

2. Do I worry others won't like me?

   Yes ☐ No ☐

3. Do I need constant approval from others?

   Yes ☐ No ☐

4. Do I appreciate myself for things other than 'success'?

   Yes ☐ No ☐

How can this help?

Many students at uni were once amongst the best in their class at school and their identity can be defined and bound up as being the best academically. At university, it isn't possible for everyone to be best in class anymore. This can feel stressful and anxiety-provoking. However, adjusting to more realistic expectations can be positive: it is possible to achieve well without having to be 'best'. It can also encourage consideration and appreciation of a much wider range of qualities that characterise the individual and are of benefit beyond study.

Considering your responses

If your responses suggest you don't value yourself sufficiently for things other than success, then it is a good time to pause and reflect on what other things you value in people and how you do, or could, demonstrate these yourself. Recognise it is possible to make mistakes, change and improve without self-hate. Let yourself feel OK about who you are.

See also Ways 39, 41, 43, 44

 To do. I will ...

Be kind to yourself

Be comfortable being you
Self-acceptance reduces stress and improves well-being.[98]

Inspect your values
Make a list of characteristics you most value in people you respect.

Focus on your positives
If you judge yourself harshly, balance this by finding some good things to say about yourself too.

Appreciate others
Appreciate the ways that other people are special. Enjoy their talents and qualities rather than over-focussing on being the most talented or gifted.

Live your values
Consider whether you exhibit the characteristics you value apart from academic success. If you do, appreciate that side of you. If not, focus on developing such qualities. Give yourself more to love and respect about yourself.

Be fair in your self-appraisal
If you have done things to others for which you should rightly feel shame, make amends and move on. Otherwise, don't focus on your imperfections.

Avoid negative comparisons
Decide what you want to achieve in real terms rather than relative to other people. Don't compare yourself negatively to anyone else.

I'm OK!

47

Use relaxation techniques

Add to your relaxation toolbox

? Do I ...?

1. Do I tense up during the day?

   Yes ☐ **No** ☐

2. Do I get headaches or a stiff neck and shoulders?

   Yes ☐ **No** ☐

3. Do I make time to relax physically and mentally?

   Yes ☐ **No** ☐

How can this help?

You can use techniques to develop a 'relaxation response' in answer to the 'stress response' described on page xii. The full body relaxation (sometimes referred to as 'body scan') and visualisation described opposite are used in many complementary therapies and other settings. Alternatively, you can learn one of several ancient practices – you get to meet people and gain a range of benefits for health and well-being. Just resting helps: people who take several waking hours away from work score higher for overall well-being.[99,100]

Considering your responses

If your responses suggest that you carry tension or stress in your body, then relaxation exercises can help. Many relaxation techniques have a calming effect on both the mind and body.

To do. I will ...

 See also Way 33

Relax body and mind

Full body relaxation

Relax flat on the floor, with your head supported on a book. Starting with your feet, tense your toes tightly, then relax them. Gain a sense of the difference. Then do the same for your feet, ankles, legs, in turn, and continue up the body, including your neck and face. Notice any areas that feel tense, or tight, and return to these again. If tension persists or keeps returning, massage the areas too.

Visualisation

Call to mind places or experiences that you find calming and safe – or just imagine a place you would like to be. It could be lying on a beach, a walk in the countryside, sailing on a lake, floating on a cloud. Focus on details in the scene to bring it to life. Imagine how it would look, sound, feel, smell. Enjoy the sensation of being there.

Yoga, Tai Chi and Qigong

These have been used for centuries and are associated with many health benefits. They help you slow down, stretch, coordinate your breathing with your movements, and focus your thoughts.[101,102,103]

Give yourself a break

Relax just by taking time away from work and study – put your feet up or get a change of scene.

Find out more

Ask at a complementary health practice or sports centre about local classes for beginners.

48

Create a calming sanctuary

Catch a tranquil moment

How can this help?

Calm can seem elusive when we are stressed, and especially in the context of a buzzing, agitating student life. Whilst stimulus is good for learning, creativity and fun, it can also drain energy, tiring us and making us more vulnerable to stress. We need a few oases of calm in the week just to unwind, settle our minds and bodies, clear our thoughts and then recharge. Creating a calm sanctuary, whether at home or in a corner of a student room, makes it easier to settle the mind for study and for relaxing afterwards.

Considering your responses

If your responses suggest that you are continually on the go in high stimulus situations, then find or create a space that helps you to unwind. Use it as a quiet retreat, ideally at least once a day.

 Do I ...?

1. Do I spend a lot of time rushing around on most days?

   Yes ☐ **No** ☐

2. Do I have a lot of stimulus and/or stimulants in my life?

   Yes ☐ **No** ☐

3. Do I have a calm space/room to which I can retreat for a while?

   Yes ☐ **No** ☐

4. Do I take calming breaks away from noise and high stimulus?

   Yes ☐ **No** ☐

 See also

Ways 14, 21, 30, 41, 49

 To do. I will ...

Find time to unwind

Create a welcoming space
Clear surfaces; throw out any rubbish; clean up. Find a comfortable chair and dim lamps. Add a plant, flowers, photos or nature pictures.

Reduce the 'buzz'
Switch off overhead lights, media, devices, alerts. Enjoy the quiet.

Remedies for calm?
Common herbal remedies and supplements used to ease stress include lemon balm, omega-3 oils, Ashwagandha.[105] Ask a pharmacist. (Speak to a doctor first if you are taking any medication.)

Use soothing aromas
There are many oils, candles and incenses to choose from. Popular choices for calm include lavender, bergamot, vetiver, neroli, orange, geranium, chamomile, ylang ylang, and sandalwood.[104]

Calming beverage
A milky drink or occasional herbal tea, such as mint or camomile (not more caffeine!)

49 **Recharge your energies**

Reboot your personal battery!

How can this help?

Stress is associated with fatigue or tiredness. This can wear you down, making it harder to find the energy to study or to think of answers to apparent difficulties. It can sap your enthusiasm for study. It is important to take time to relax in order to recoup your energy. This can be through many different routes, so it is good to use a varied menu to restore body and mind and raise your spirits.

Considering your responses

If your responses suggest that you are getting tired because of stress, or stressed because you are tired, devise a menu of ways to refresh and re-energise yourself throughout the day. If tiredness doesn't have an obvious cause or persists, get a check-up from a medical practitioner.

 See also Ways 21, 30, 41, 47, 48

(?) **Do I ...?**

1. Do I feel tired a lot?
   Yes ☐ **No** ☐

2. Do I create time just for relaxing?
   Yes ☐ **No** ☐

3. Do I take steps to recharge my energy?
   Yes ☐ **No** ☐

4. Do I use varied ways of energising myself throughout the day?
   Yes ☐ **No** ☐

 To do. I will ...

Vary your menu for restoring energy

Take plenty of breaks

… if you are studying or working hard, to help you re-energise.

Rehydrate

Dehydration adds to stress. Drinking water throughout the day helps relaxation and restores physical and mental energy.[106]

Green tea

Green tea has a good balance of caffeine and antioxidants, and is associated with good health, calm and mental relaxation.[107]

Play

Just have fun. Play a game. Spend time with your children. Do something creative.

A relaxing bath

… or a refreshing shower. Take your time. Add a fragrant bubble bath so it feels like a treat.

Eat well; take snacks

Eat nourishing rather than junk food to maintain energy for longer.

Relax your eyes

Rub your palms together to generate heat. Place palms over your open eyes for a few minutes to refresh them.

Lavender oil

Rub a few drops into your hands. Massage into hands, feet and temples. Or just inhale the fumes to calm the mind.

Inspire yourself

Daydream, read or listen to something that inspires ideas and raises your spirits.

50

Enjoy a little distraction

Take time out from worrying!

How can this help?

Distracting yourself won't necessarily solve your problems, but it can give you a break from them. That can help you to reduce stress levels and ease feelings of anxiety. Giving the brain downtime to relax enables it to think more clearly and to come up with solutions. Many forms of relaxation have soothing effects or raise mood. In general, whatever the cause of your stress, it is good to have time for yourself and to enjoy life to the full.

Considering your responses

If your responses suggest that you don't give yourself a break from your worries, then plan some time just for you into each day. Give yourself something to look forward to. If you need inspiration, consider the activities opposite that other people report using when stressed.

 See also Ways 14, 19, 24, 49

(?) Do I ...?

1. Do I feel it is risky to give myself a break from my worries?

   Yes **No**

2. Do I find time just for me most days?

   Yes **No**

3. Do I have things I can do to divert myself when I am stressed?

   Yes **No**

 To do. I will …

Try out some of the things other people do ...

- Board games
- Soaking in the bath
- Baking
- Changing the furniture round
- Cooking a delicious meal
- Sudoku puzzles
- Codeword puzzles
- Reading a book
- Watching films
- Playing a game with their children
- Petting animals
- Walking the dog
- Being creative: making something
- Skyping family
- Gardening

- Tidying up
- Tai Chi or Qigong
- Martial Arts
- Swimming
- Riding a bike
- Reading magazines
- Listening to music
- Helping out in the student union
- Sports clubs
- Joining a student society
- Watching cat videos
- Growing a plant
- Planning a holiday
- Window shopping.

Other things I could do ...

Habits shaper: Track your good intentions

Draw together your entries from the 'I will' boxes. Jot down the page number for easy cross reference. Select those you are keenest to do. Add a star, emoticon or **highlighting** each time you act on your intention.

I have committed to doing ...	Way	Page
☺		
☺		
☺		
☺		

I have committed to doing ...	Way	Page
☺		
☺		
☺		
☺		
☺		

My progress so far

Keep track of which of these 50 Ways you have started and completed (✔). If you come back to the book after a break, you can see at a glance which aspects you had intended to pursue, and decide whether to take up from where you left off.

Way	Page	Short title	Doing	Done!
1	2	Appreciate 'helpful stress'		
2	4	Harness the benefits of stress		
3	6	Know the signs of excess stress		
4	10	Recognise your own stress triggers		
5	12	Take signs of stress seriously		
6	14	Take charge!		
7	16	Get physical!		
8	18	Talk it through!		
9	20	Get enough (good) sleep		
10	22	Combat homesickness		
11	24	Laugh more!		
12	26	Get well organised		
13	28	Practise mindfulness		
14	30	Get outdoors into nature		
15	32	Watch nature on screen		
16	34	Know your limits		
17	36	Start the day right!		
18	38	Make time work for you		
19	40	Get social!		
20	42	Take stress out of meeting new people		
21	44	Music to your ears!		
22	46	Park your troubles!		

Way	Page	Short title	Doing	Done!
23	48	Create a realistic study schedule		
24	50	Change scene and break routine		
25	52	Relax with breathing exercises		
26	54	Develop good study skills and habits		
27	56	Write it out		
28	58	Sort your finances		
29	60	Take a walk!		
30	62	Eat good mood food		
31	64	Devise a good exam strategy		
32	66	Manage your 'mind exposure'		
33	68	Relax jaw and fists		
34	70	Avoid task-switching stress		
35	72	Benefit from the power of touch		
36	74	Trigger the 'happy' chemicals		
37	76	Reduce the pressure on assignment deadlines		
38	78	Make decisions		
39	80	Accept your emotions		
40	82	Change your relationship with social media		
41	84	Express yourself creatively		
42	86	Help someone else		
43	88	Befriend your mistakes		
44	90	Cultivate a balanced perspective		
45	92	Have a good cry!		
46	94	Accept yourself		
47	96	Use relaxation techniques		
48	98	Create a calming sanctuary		
49	100	Recharge your energies		
50	102	Enjoy a little distraction		

List of 20+ things I appreciate, enjoy or am grateful for ...

List at least 20 things you enjoy, appreciate or feel gratitude for – about your life study, your course, and your learning.

1

2

3

4

5

6

7

8

9

10

11

12

13

14

15

16

17

18

19

20

Where to find out more

Apps

Calm www.calm.com/ (Calming images and meditations)

Student Health App www.expertselfcare.com/health-apps/student-health-app/ (From the University of Bristol.) Covers a range of health and mental issues relevant to students.

Daskal, L. (2016). *13 Of the Best Apps to Manage Your Stress* www.inc.com/lolly-daskal/13-of-the-best-apps-to-manage-stress.html

Books

DK (2017). *Stress: The Psychology of Managing Pressure* (New York: Penguin Random House)

Kempton, B. (2018). *Wabi Sabi: Japanese Wisdom for a Perfectly Imperfect Life* (London: Piatkus)

Creative activity books

There is a large range of books available for creative activities to promote pausing for rest, relaxation and reflection. Below are some popular titles.

Elsharouni, C. (2017). *Adult Coloring Book: Stress Relieving Designs, Animals, Mandalas, Flowers, Paisley Patterns And So Much More: Coloring Book For Adults* (USA: Selah Works Prints).

Mind (2017). *The Wellbeing Journal: Creative Activities to Inspire* (London: Michael O'Mara).

Moore, G. (2016). *The Mindfulness Puzzle Book, Relaxing Puzzles to De-stress and Unwind* (London: Robinson).

Crisis support

National Health Service, UK www.nhs.uk/Service-Search/Psychological-therapies-(IAPT)/LocationSearch/10008

Nightline www.nightline.ac.uk/

Samaritans www.samaritans.org/how-we-can-help-you

Health and fitness

https://apps.beta.nhs.uk/ Wide range of free apps from the NHS on many aspects of health

Exercise

www.brokeandhealthy.com/ (100 free or cheap ways to exercise)

www.yogajournal.com/

www.beginnerstaichi.com/

www.exercisetoheal.com

Eating well on a budget

www.nhs.uk/live-well/eat-well/eight-tips-for-healthy-eating/

Sheppard, A. (2017). *The Savvy Shopper's Cookbook* (Ebury Digital).

Many supermarkets provide free seasonal recipes and meal-planners on their websites, and often offer deals on ingredients.

Health

www.nhs.uk/live-well/healthy-body/getting-medical-care-as-a-student/

www.everydayhealth.com/

www.healthline.com/

www.mindbodygreen.com/food

International students

www.ukcisa.org.uk/ (Advice and information for international students in the UK)

www.foreignstudents.com/health/nhs

Managing money

Advice and information

www.ucas.com/finance/managing (UCAS)

www.moneyadviceservice.org.uk/en (Money Advice Service)

International Students in UK

international.studentcalculator.org/further-information/banking/login_form

Practical tips and resources

Macmillan Student Planner (Cottrell, S.). Updated annually.

Opening a UK bank account

Leaflet to download at bba.org.uk/International Students. (British Banking Association – now part of UKfinance.org.uk)

Sharia banking in UK

moneyadviceservice.org.uk/Sharia-compliant savings

Mental health/stress

www.mentalhealth.org.uk

www.mind.org.uk

www.nhs.uk/choices (Student Stress: self-help tips. Includes links to 8 free mental well-being podcasts or audio guides)

www.nhs.uk/conditions/stress-anxiety-depression/ways-relieve-stress/

www.samaritans.org/education/deal/coping-strategies/managing-stress

www.sane.org.uk (Mental health emotional support services, offers support, helpline, textcare, support forum and blog to share experience)

www.studentminds.org.uk/findsupport.html (Student Mind – support for mental health concerns)

Twitter

@StudentMindsOrg

#StudentMindsBlog

Mindfulness

Cottrell, S. (2018). *Mindfulness for Students* (London: Red Globe Press).

Online meditations at: www.macmillanihe.com/mindfulness

Twitter

#mindful #mindfulness #mindfulstudent

Relaxation

General information

www.mind.org.uk/information-support/tips-for-everyday-living/relaxation/#.W9qvxXv7Spo

www.verywellfit.com/relaxing-total-body-stretches-1231150 (Eight relaxing body stretches, with videos)

Nature video and programmes

Another World (4K free video) www.youtube.com/watch?v=Bey4XXJAqS8

Breathtaking Colours of Nature (free video) www.youtube.com/watch?v=RK1K2bCg4J8

Natural World (BBC 2018) www.bbc.co.uk/programmes/b09z77yq

https://videos.pexels.com/search/nature (wide range of free short nature videos)

https://pixabay.com/en/videos/list/?cat=nature (free short nature videos)

Relaxing sounds

https://lusity.en.uptodown.com/android (Relaxing sounds for calm, rest and sleep.)

https://itunes.apple.com/us/app/relaxing-sounds-nature-lite/id345747251?mt=8 (Relaxing Nature Sounds) (Red Hammer Software; Free for IOS devices)

Self-massage

my Physio SA (2016) How to self-massage tight and sore jaw muscles (31/1/2016) www.youtube.com/watch?v=PedbSROD6wE

www.csp.org.uk/public-patient/rehabilitation-exercises/shoulder-pain (Shoulders)

www.csp.org.uk/publications/neck-pain-exercises (Neck)

Sleep

Breus, M. J. (2017). 5 'Relaxation Techniques for Better Sleep' (1/1/2017). Psychology Today

www.psychologytoday.com/us/blog/sleep-newzzz/201701/5-relaxation-techniques-better-sleep

Huffington, A. (2010). 'How to Succeed? Get more sleep'. TEDWomen 2010. TED conferences.

www.nhs.uk/live-well/sleep-and-tiredness/10-tips-to-beat-insomnia/

Support Groups

Your college or university support services can advise you of groups where you can share experiences with other students, either that they run themselves, or in the locality. Other people likely to know of useful groups are: your doctor, local medical practices, college chaplains, religious organisations and confidential helplines.

Study skills

Books

Cottrell, S. (2019). *The Study Skills Handbook* (5th edn) (London: Red Globe Press).

Cottrell, S. (2014). *Dissertations and Project Reports* (London: Red Globe Press).

Free website

Macmillan free study skills site: www.thestudyspace.com

Twitter

@cottrell_study

#SuccessfulStudent

#StudyTip

#amlearning

Time management

Cottrell, S. (updated annually). *The Macmillan Student Planner*. (London: Red Globe Press). (For organising all aspects of life as a student and planning your time.)

Cottrell, S. (2019). *50 Ways to Manage Time Effectively* (London: Red Globe Press).

References and bibliography

1. NHS (2018). [online] Available at: www.nhs.uk/Service-Search/Psychologicaltherapies-(IAPT)/LocationSearch/10008
2. Student Minds (2018). [online] Available at: www.studentminds.org.uk/findsupport.html
3. Scott, E. (2018). *Why do Stressors Affect People Differently?* [online] Available at: www.verywellmind.com/why-do-stressors-affect-people-differently-3145061 [Accessed 27 August 2018].
4. Lazarus, R. S. and Folkman, S. (1984). *Stress, Appraisal and Coping* (New York: Springer Publishing Company).
5. McGonigal, K. (2015). *The Upside of Stress: Why stress is Good For You, and How to Get Good at it* (2nd edn) (New York: Avery).
6. Essel, G. and Owusu, P. (2017). *Causes of students' stress, its effects on their academic success, and stress management by students.* Case Study at Seinajoki University of Applied Sciences, Finland. [online] Available at: theseus.fi [Accessed 28 Sept 2017].
7. National Union of Students (2015). Mental health poll, November 2015. [online] Available at: www.nusconnect.org.uk/resources/mental-health-poll-2015 [Accessed 28 February 2019].
8. YouthSight (2013). *Psychological Distress in the UK Student Population: Prevalence, Timing and Accessing Support.* Final research findings. [online] Available at: www.nightline.ac.uk/wp-content/uploads/2014/08/Psychological-distress-prevalence-timings-accessing-support-Aug-2014.pdf [Accessed 28 February 2019].
9. UPP (2017). *Annual Student Experience Study 2017.* [online] Available at: www.upp-ltd.com/student-survey/ [Accessed 28 February 2019].
10. NUS-USI (2017). Student Wellbeing Research Report, [online] Available at: www.nusconnect.org.uk/resources/nus-usi-student-wellbeing-research-report-2017 [Accessed 10 October 2017].
11. George Dimitrov, B. E. (2017). 'A study on the impact of Academic Stress among college students in India'. *Ideal Research, An International Multidisciplinary e-Journal,* 2(4).
12. Nandrajog, S. (2018). 'Are Indian Colleges Equipped To Deal With Students' Mental Health Issues?' Campus Watch. 26 May. [online] Available at: www.youthkiawaaz.com/2018/05/mental-health-situation-in-indian-colleges/[Accessed 20 August 2018].
13. Ross, S. E., Neibling, B. C. and Heckert, T. M. (1999). 'Sources of stress among college students'. *College Student Journal,* 33(2), pp. 312–17.
14. Kadison, R. and Di Geronimo, T. F. (2004). *College of the overwhelmed: The campus mental health crisis and what to do about it* (San Francisco: Jossey-Bass).
15. Kim, K-I, Won, H., Liu, X., Liu, P. and Kitanishi, K. (1997). 'Students' Stress in China, Japan and Korea: a Transcultural Study'. *International Journal of Social Psychiatry,* 43(2), pp. 87–94.
16. Ang, P. L. D. and Liamputtong, P. (2008). '"Out of the Circle": International students and the use of university counselling services'. *Journal of Research in International Education,* 5, pp. 131–54.

17. Yi, J. K., Lin, J.-C. G. and Kishimoto, Y. (2003). 'Utilization of counseling services by international students'. *Journal of Instructional Psychology, 30*, pp. 333–42.

18. Zhang, N. and Dixon, D. N. (2003). 'Acculturation and attitudes of Asian international students toward seeking psychological help'. *Journal of Multicultural Counseling & Development, 31*, pp. 205–22.

19. Bataineh, D. (2013). 'Academic Stress among Undergraduate students: the case of Education faculty at King Saud University'. *International Interdisciplinary Journal of Education, 2*(1).

20. Elizabeth, M. S. (2012). 'Stress In College: Common Causes of Stress In College'. *Medical Review Board.* [online] Available at: http://stress.about.com/od/ studentstress/a/stress_college.htm

21. Brown, P. (2016). 'The invisible problem? Improving students' mental health'. *Higher Education Policy Institute HEPI Report 88.* At hepi.ac.uk. [Accessed 9 October 2017].

22. Thorley, C. (2017). *Not by degrees: Improving student mental health in the UK's universities* (London, IPPR). [online] Available at: www.ippr.org/research/publications/ not-by-degrees

23. Business Today (2018). *9 out of 10 Indians suffer from stress.* [online] Available at: www.businesstoday.in/lifestyle/off-track/indians-suffer-from-stress-depression/story/ 280119.html [Accessed 28 February 2019].

24. China Daily (2012). *Living with stress.* [online] Available at: www.chinadaily.com.cn/ china/2012-12/12/content_16009304.htm [Accessed 28 February 2019].

25. American Psychological Association (2015). *Stress in America – Paying with our health.* [online] Available at: www.apa.org/news/press/releases/stress/2014/stress-report.pdf [Accessed 27 August 2018].

26. Forth (2018). *Great Britain and Stress – How bad is it and why is it happening?.* [online] Available at: www.forthwithlife.co.uk/blog/great-britain-and-stress [Accessed 27 August 2018].

27. Vogelzangs, N., Beekman, A. T., Milaneschi, Y., Bandinelli, S., Ferucci, L. and Pennix, B. W. (2010). 'Urinary cortisol and six-year risk of all-cause and cardiovascular mortality'. *Journal of Clinical Endocrinal Metabolism*, 95(11), pp. 4959–64.

28. Australian Psychological Society (2015). *Stress & Wellbeing – how Australians are coping with life.* [online] Available at: www.headsup.org.au/docs/defaultsource/ default-document-library/stress-and-wellbeing-in-australiareport.pdf?sfvrsn=7f08274d_4 [Accessed 27 August 2018].

29. VanKim, N. A. and Nelson, T. F. (2013). 'Vigorous physical activity, mental health, perceived stress and socialising among college students'. *American Journal of Health Promotion*, (28), pp. 7–15.

30. Shankar, N. L. and Park, C. L. (2016). 'Effects of Stress on students' physical and mental health and academic success'. *International Journal of School and Educational Psychology*, 4(1), part 1, pp. 5–9.

31. National Health Service (2018). *Find psychological therapies (IAPT) services.* [online] Available at: www.nhs.uk/Service-Search/Psychological-therapies-(IAPT)/ LocationSearch/10008 [Accessed 27 August 2018].

32. Student Minds (2018). *Find Support.* [online] Available at: www.studentminds.org.uk/ findsupport.html [Accessed 27 August 2018].

33. Stults-Kolehmainen, M. A. and Sinha, R. (2014). 'The Effects of Stress on Physical Activity and Exercise'. *Sports. Med.* January, 44(1), pp. 81–121.

34. Milam, E. *Deskercise!* (2014). *33 Smart Ways to Exercise at Work*, 28 May. Available at: https://greatist.com/fitness/deskercise-33-ways-exercise-work [Accessed 28 February 2019].

35. Hershner, S. D. and Chervin, R. D. (2014). 'Causes and consequences of sleepiness among college students'. *Nature and the Science of Sleep*, 6, pp. 73–84.

36. Nightline Association (2013). *Depressed, anxious, lonely and homesick: Study reveals darker side to student life.* [online] Available at: www.nightline.ac.uk/sites/default/files/Nightline-YouthSight%20Results.pdf [Accessed 27 August 2018].

37. Berk, L. S., Tan, S. A. and Dottie Berk, D. (2008). 'Cortisol and Catecholamine stress hormone decrease is associated with the behavior of perceptual anticipation of mirthful laughter'. *The FASEB Journal*, 22:946.11.

38. Murray, M. (2009). *Laughter is the Best Medicine for your Heart.* Umm.edu. Released 14 July 2009. University of Maryland. [Accessed 13 Sept 2017].

39. Cottrell, S. (updated annually). *The Macmillan Student Planner* (London: Red Globe Press).

40. Cottrell, S. (2019). *The Study Skills Handbook* (5th edn) (London: Red Globe Press).

41. Levy, D. M., Wobbrock, J. O., Kasniak, A. W. and Ostergren, M. (2012). 'The Effects of Mindfulness Meditation Training on Multitasking in a High-Stress Information Environment'. *Proceedings of Graphics Interface*, pp. 45–52.

42. Lazar, S. W., Kerr, C. E., Wasserman, R. H., Gray, J. H., Greve, D. N., Treadway, M. N., McGarvey, M., Quinn, B. T., Dusek, J. A., Benson, H., Rausch, S. L., Moore, C. I. and Fischl, B. (2005). 'Meditation experience is associated with increased cortical thickness'. *Neuro Report* 16(17), pp. 1893–7.

43. Cottrell, S. (2018). *Mindfulness for Students* (London: Red Globe Press).

44. *The Real Happiness Project* (2017) by BBC Earth and Dacher Keltner from the University of California, Berkeley. [online] Available at: www.realhappinessproject.com. [Accessed 28 February 2019].

45. Brown, D. K., Barton, J. L. and Gladwell, V. F. (2013). 'Viewing Nature Scenes Positively Affects Recovery of Autonomic Function Following Acute-Mental Stress'. *Environmental Science & Technology*, 47(11), pp. 5562–9.

46. Rothbard, N. and Wilk, S. (2011). 'Waking up on the Right or Wrong side of the Bed: Start-of-Workday-Mood, Work Events, Employee Affect, And Performance'. *Academy of Management Journal*, 54(5), pp. 959–80.

47. Misra, R. and McKean, M. (2000). 'College Students' Academic Stress and its relation to their anxiety, time-management, and leisure satisfaction'. *American Journal of Health Studies*, 16(1).

48. Campbell, R. L. and Svenson, L. W. (1992). 'Perceived level of stress among university undergraduate students in Edmonton, Canada'. *Perceptual and Motor Skills*, 75(2), pp. 552–4.

49. Novotney, A. (2013). 'Music as medicine'. *Monitor on Psychology American Psychological Association*, 44(10), p. 46.

50. Burns, J., Labbe, E., Williams, K. and McCall, J. (1999). 'Perceived and physiological indicators of relaxation: as different as Mozart and Alice in Chains'. *Applied Psychophysical Biofeedback*, Sept, 24(3) pp. 197–202.

51. Thorma, M. V., La Maarca, R., Bronnimann, R., Finkel, L., Ehlert, U. and Nater, U.M. (2013). 'The Effect of Music on the Human Stress Response', Newton R. L. (ed), *PLoS ONE*, 2013, 8(8): e70156. doi:10.1371/journal.pone.0070156

52. Schwabe, L. and Wold, O. T. (2009). 'Stress Prompts Habit Behavior in Humans'. *Journal of Neuroscience*, 3 June, 29(22), pp. 7191–8.

53. Bedewy, D. and Gabriel, A. (2015). 'Examining Perceptions of academic stress and its sources amongst university students: The Perception of Academic Stress Scale'. *Health Psychology Open*, July, 2(2).

54. Shah, M., Hasan, S., Malik, S. et al. (2010). 'Perceived stress, sources and severity of stress among medical undergraduates in a Pakistani medical school'. *BMC Medical Education*, 10, p. 2.

55. Sohail, N. (2013). 'Stress and academic performance among medical students'. *Journal of the College of Physicians and Surgeons Pakistan*, 23, pp. 67–71.

56. Harikiran, A., Srinagesh, J., Nagesh, K. et al. (2012). 'Perceived sources of stress amongst final year dental under-graduate students in a dental teaching institution in Bangalore, India: A cross-sectional study'. *Indian Journal of Dental Research*, 23, pp. 331–6.

57. Lynton, H. and Salovey, P. (1997). 'The effects of mood on expository writing. Imagination'. *Cognition and Personality*, 17(2), pp. 95–110.

58. Kerner, E. A. and Fitzpatrick, M. R. (2007). 'Integrating writing into psychotherapy practice: a matrix of change processes and structural dimensions'. *Psychotherapy: Theory, Research, Practice, Training*, 44(3), pp. 333–46.

59. Lepore, S. J. and Smyth, J. M. (eds) (2002). 'The writing cure: How expressive writing promotes health and emotional well-being' (Washington, DC: American Psychological Association).

60. Ramirez, G. and Beilock, S. L. (2011). 'Writing about testing worries boosts exam performance in the classroom'. *Science*, 331, pp. 211–13.

61. Murray, B. (2002). 'Writing to Heal'. *Monitor on Psychology* (American Psychological Association), June, 33(6), apa.org. Print version, p. 54.

62. Mckinney, F. (1976). 'Free writing as therapy'. *Psychotherapy: Theory, Research, Practice, Training*, 13(2), pp. 183–7.

63. Pennebaker, J. W., Colder, M. and Sharp, L. K. (1990). 'Accelerating the coping process'. *Journal of Personality and Social Psychology*, 58(3), pp. 528–37.

64. National Union of Students (2016). *NUS report for Future Finance* (2016), Infographic: Money on my mind, 5 May. [Accessed 10 October 2017].

65. The Ohio State University – Centre for Student Life (2015). *National Student Finances Wellness Study*. [online] Available at: https://cssl.osu.edu/posts/documents/nsfws-national-descriptive-report.pdf [Accessed 27 August 2018].

66. Schoenfeld, T. J., Rada, P., Pieruzzini, P. R., Hsueh, B. and Gould, E. (2013). 'Physical Exercise Prevents Stress-Induced Activation of Granule Neurons and Enhances Local Inhibitory Mechanisms in the Dentate Gyrus'. *The Journal of Neuroscience*, 33(18), pp. 7770–7.

67. Aubrey, A. (2014). *Food-mood connection: How you eat can amp up or tamp down stress*. [online] 14 July. [online] Available at: https://hms.harvard.edu/news/food-mood-connection-how-you-eat-can-amp-or-tamp-down-stress [Accessed 28 February 2019].

68. Hibbeln, J. (2007). 'From Homicide to Happiness – A Commentary on Omega-3 Fatty Acids in Human Society'. *Nutrition and Health*, 19(1), pp. 9–19.

69. Steptoe, A., Gibson, E. L., Vounonvirta, R. et al. (2007). 'The effects of tea on psychophysiological stress responsivity and post-stress recovery: a randomised double-blind trial'. *Psychopharmacology*, 90(1), pp. 81–9.

70. Sasaki-Otomaru, A., Sakuma, Y., Mochizuki, Y., Ishida, S., Kanoya, Y. and Sato, C. (2011). 'Effect of Regular Gum Chewing on Levels of Anxiety, Mood, and Fatigue in Healthy Young Adults'. *Clinical Practice and Epidemiology in Mental Health*, 7, pp. 33–139.

71. Nishigawa, K., Suzuki, Y. and Matsuka, Y. (2015). 'Masticatory performance alters stress relief effect of gum chewing'. *Journal of Prosthodontic Research*, 59(4), pp. 262–7.

72. Hashmat, S., Hashmat, M., Amanullah, F. and Aziz, S. (2008). 'Factors causing exam anxiety in medical students'. *The Journal of Pakistan Medical Association*, 58(4), pp. 67–170.

73. Cottrell, S. (2012). *The Exam Skills Handbook* (2nd edn) (London: Red Globe Press).

74. Hasan, Y., Begue, L. and Bushman, B. J. (2013). 'Violent Video Games Stress People Out and Make Them More Aggressive'. *Aggressive Behaviour*, vol. 9, pp. 64–70.

75. Stone, L. (2009). *Beyond Simple Multi-tasking: Continuous Partial Attention* [Blog] on Lindastone.net. n.p., November 2009.

76. Willingham, D. T. (2010). 'Have Technology and Multitasking Rewired How Students Learn?'. *American Educator*, 34(2), pp. 23–8.

77. Calderwell, C., Ackerman, P. L. and Conklin, E. M. (2014). 'What Else Do College Students "Do" Whilst Studying. An Investigation of Multitasking'. *Computers and Education*, 75, pp. 9–29.

78. Ophir, E., Nass, C. and Wagner, A. D. (2009). 'Cognitive control in media multitaskers'. *Proceedings of the National Academy of Sciences of the United States of America*, 106(35), pp. 15583–7.

79. Korb, A. (2015). *Upward Spiral: Using Neuroscience to Reverse the Course of Depression, One Small Change at a Time* (Oakland: New Harbinger Publications).

80. Breuning, L. G. (2016). *Habits of a Happy Brain. Retrain your Brain to Boost Your Serotonin, Dopamine, Oxytocin and Endorphin levels* (Avon MA, USA: Adams Media).

81. Tice, D. M. and Baumeister, R. F. (1997). 'Longitudinal Study of Procrastination, Performance, Stress, and Health: The Costs and Benefits of Dawdling'. *Psychological Science*, 6(8), pp. 454–8.

82. Howard, C. D., Li, H., Geddes, C. E. and Jin, X. (2017). 'Dynamic Nigrostriatal Dopamine Biases Action Selection'. *Neuron*, 93(6), pp. 1436–50.

83. Olivo, E. (2015). 'Why Acceptance is One of the Best Stress Reducers'. [online] Available at: www.psychologytoday.com/gb/blog/wise-mind-living/201501/why-acceptance-is-one-the-best-stress-reducers Posted 2 January 2015. [Accessed 17 October 2017].

84. Ford, B. Q., Lam, P., John, O. P. and Mauss, I. B. (2017). 'The Psychological Health Benefits of Accepting Negative Emotional Thoughts: Laboratory, Diary and Longitudinal Evidence'. *Journal of Personality and Social Psychology*, 13 Jul. [online] Doi: 10.1037/pspp0000157. epub ahead of print.

85. Rock, D. (2009). *Your Brain at Work: Strategies for overcoming distraction, retaining focus and working smarter all day long* (New York: Harper Business).

86. Kross, E., Verduyn, P., Demiralp, E., Park, J., Lee, D. S., Lin, N., Shablack, H., Jonides, J. and Ybarra, O. (2013). 'Facebook Use Predicts Declines in Subjective Wellbeing in Young Adults', *PLoS ONE* 8(8): e69841. https://doi.org/10.1371/journal.pone.0069841

87. Taylor, C. (2011). 'For Millennials, social media is not all fun and games'. *GigaOM*. April 29. [online] Available at: https://gigaom.com/2011/04/29/millennial-mtv-study/ [Accessed 28 February 2019].

88. Rosen, L. D., Carrier, L. M. and Cheever, N. A. (2013). 'Facebook and texting made me do it: media-induced task-switching while studying'. *Computers in Human behavior*, 29, pp. 948–58.

89. Amabile, T. M. and Kramer, S. J. (2011). *The Progress Principle – Using small wins to ignite joy, engagement and creativity at work* (Cambridge: Harvard Business Review Press).

90. Kaufman, S. B. (2015). 'The Creative Life and Well-being'. [Blog] *Scientific American. com*. [Accessed 16 October 2017].

91. Santos, E. (2014). *Coloring Isn't Just for Kids. It Can Actually Help Adults Combat Stress.* The Huffington Post, 14 October 2014.

92. Arnetz, B. B., Lewalski, P., Arnetz, J., Breejen, K. and Przyklenk, K. (2017). 'Examining self-reported and biological stress and near misses among Emergency Medicine residents: a single-centre cross-sectional assessment in the USA'. *BMJ Open*, 7:e016479

93. Antony, M. M. and Swinson, R. P. (2009). *When Perfect isn't Good Enough* (2nd edn) (Oakland: New Harbinger Publications).

94. Brennan, M. (2017). *It's All About Perspective. Living a Balanced Life.* [online] Available at: blogs.psychcentral.com [Accessed 18 October 2017].

95. Leahy, R. L. (2017). 'Putting Things in Perspective. Five easy steps to reducing daily stress'. *Psychology Today*, Posted 27 February 2017. [Accessed 18 October 2017].

96. Frey, W. H. (1985). *Crying: The Mystery of Tears* (Minneapolis, MN: Winston Press).

97. Gracanin, A., Bylsma, L. M. and Vingerhoets, Ad. J. J. M. (2014). 'Is crying selfsoothing?' *Frontiers in Psychology*, 5, p. 502.

98. Pillay, S. (2016). 'Greater Self-acceptance improves emotional well-being', *Harvard Health Publishing*. Harvard Medical School. [online] Available at: www.health.harvard. edu/blog/greater-self-acceptance-improves-emotional-well-201605169546 [Accessed 28 February 2019]. [Accessed 17 October 2017].

99. Durham University News (2016). *Rest and well-being – world's largest survey* (27 September 2016) [online] Available at: www.dur.ac.uk/news/newsitem/?itemno=28980 [Accessed 24 August 2018].

100. BBC The Anatomy of Rest. *Finding Rest in the Modern World: The rest test results.* [online] Available at: www.bbc.co.uk/programmes/b07w0s5l. [Accessed 24 August 2018].

101. See online exercise site: www.yogajournal.com

102. See online exercise site: www.beginnerstaichi.com

103. See online exercise site: www.exercisetoheal

104. Wong, C. (2017). *Essential oils help ease stress.* [online] Available at: www.verywellmind.com/essential-oils-to-help-ease-stress-89636 [Accessed 27 August 2018].

105. Mentalhealthfood.com (2017). 'Herbal remedies for depression and anxiety'. [online] Available at: https://mentalhealthfood.net/13-herbs-for-treating-depression-andanxiety [online] [Accessed 27 August 2018].

106. Shaw, G. (2009). *Water and stress reduction: sipping stress away.* [online] Available at: www.webmd.com/diet/features/water-stress-reduction#1 [Accessed 27 August 2018].

107. Unno, K., Noda, S., Kawasaki, Y., Yamada, H., Morita, A., Iguchi, K. and Nakamura, Y. (2017). 'Reduced Stress and Improved Sleep Quality Caused by Green Tea Are Associated with a Reduced Caffeine Content'. *Nutrients*, 9(7), p. 777.

108. Cottrell, S. (2019). *50 Ways to Manage Time Effectively* (London: Red Globe Press).

Bibliography

1. Harris, S. (2014). 'The Power of the Nap'. Psychology Today, 18 February. [online] Available at: www.psychologytoday.com/us/blog/the-land-nod/201402/thepower-the-nap [Accessed 27 August 2018].

2. NPR/Robert Wood Johnson Foundation/Harvard School of Public Health (2014). *The Burden of Stress in America.* [online] Available at: www.rwjf.org/content/dam/farm/reports/surveys_and_polls/2014/rwjf414295 [Accessed 27 August 2018].

3. Kempton, M. J., Ettinger, U. and Foster, R. (2011). 'Dehydration affects brain structure and function in healthy adolescents'. *Human Brain Mapping*, 32(1), pp. 71–9.

4. Neves, J. and Hillman, N. (2017). *Student Academic Experience Survey 2017* (Higher Education Academy and Higher Education Policy Institute). [online] Available at: www.hepi.ac.uk/wp-content/uploads/2017/06/2017-Student-Academic-Experience-Survey-Final-Report.pdf [Accessed 28 February 2019].

5. Student Minds (2014).*Grand Challenges in Student Mental Health.* [online] Available at: www.studentminds.org.uk/uploads/3/7/8/4/3784584/grand_challenges_report_for_public.pdf. [Accessed 28 February 2019].

6. Unite Students (2016). *Student Resilience: Unite Students Insight Report.* [online] Available at: www.unite-group.co.uk/sites/default/files/2017-03/studentinsight-report-2016 [Accessed 28 February 2019].

7. YouGov (2016). *One in four students suffer from mental health problems*, 9, August 2016. [online] Available at: yougov.co.uk/news/2016/08/09/quarterbritains-students-are-afflicted-mentalhea/ [Accessed 28 February 2019].

Index

Academic pressures xiii, xv, 54–5
Acceptance – emotions, self 80–1, 88–9, 94–5
Action lists 15, 89
Addiction xv
Adrenaline xii, 3, 16, 76
Age-related stress xv
Aggression 8, 69, 92
Alcohol xiv, xv, xvii, 15
'All-nighters' xiv, 21
Anger 81
Animals 73
Anxiety x, xi, xviii, xix, xxi, 12, 16, 28, 47, 63, 66, 67, 72, 80, 94
Appreciation 2–3, 94, 95, 108–9
Apps 17, 110
Aromas 99
Ashwagandha 99, 120
Aspirations 34–5
Assignments xiii, xv, 13, 76–7, 88–9
Attention, paying xviii, 20–1, 29, 70–1

Balanced approach 3, 5, 19, 23, 34, 45, 46–7, 49, 66–7, 88–9, 90–1
BDNF 16
Bedtime blues xix, 66–7 (see also Sleep)
Behaviours 8
Belonging 75

Benefits of stress xii, 2–5
Bereavement xvi, 10, 18, 80
Blood pressure xii, 8
Body scan 96
Boredom 50
Brain xii, xviii, 49, 51, 70, 74, 81
Breaks 17, 49, 61, 97, 101, 102–3
Breathing exercises 52–3

Caffeine xiv, 20, 21
Calm xvii, xix, x, 28–9, 44, 53, 72, 78, 96–9
Catastrophising 67, 90
Challenge xiii, xx, 4–5, 34–5
Change, coping with xiii, xvi, 10, 22–3
Change, making a change x, 50–1, 61, 81, 82–3
Chemicals xii, xvii, 70, 74–5
Chewing gum 63
Chocolate 63
Choices ix, 15, 50, 78–9
Choir 45
Clutter (see De-clutter)
Cognition xvii
Colouring 84
Commitment ix, x
Community groups 17, 87
Community, sense of 87

Concentration xviii, xix, xxi, 3, 8, 71
Confidence xx, 40–3, 65
Confidentiality xxii, xxiii, 18, 57
Contentment 32
Control xiii, xx, xxiii, 2
Taking charge 10–15
Coping mechanisms/ strategies x, 15
Cortisol xvii, xviii, 24, 92
Creative expression xviii, xxiii, 30, 50, 84–5, 103, 110
Crisis support 110
Critical appraisal 88, 89, 91
Criticism 89
Crying 8, 92–3
Cycles xix, xx, 88

Dance 16–17
Decision-making xviii, xxi, xxii, 8, 15, 78–9
Deadlines xiii, 36–7, 76–7
De-clutter 26–7, 99
Dehydration 93, 101
Denial/dismissal xxii, 8, 12–13, 19, 23, 80, 93
Diary skills 39, 113
Digestion xvii
Discovery, importance of 75
Discrimination xvi

Distraction xviii, 48, 102–3
Dopamine xvii, 75
Dread, sense of xvii, 8

Eating patterns/ disorders xv, xxi, 7, 8
Eating well xxiii, xiv, xv, 7, 111
Eating with others 23, 41, 51, 59
Emotional energy 91
Emotions xvii, xxi, 30, 32–3, 56, 80–1
Endorphins 16, 75
Energy, low energy xix, 62
Energy, recharging xii, xx, 2–5, 26–7, 100–1
Enjoyment 8, 17, 23, 24–5, 30–1, 54, 65, 75, 84–5, 96–103, 108–9
Exams xiii, xv, 13, 64–5, 90
Excitement xi, xii, 3, 5
Exercise xxi, 14–15, 64, 75, 113
Expectations, realistic 13, 34–5
Experience, making sense of 56–7

Failure, fear of xvii, xix, xxi, 5, 9, 54
Family xv, xvi, xx, xxi, 19, 22–3
Fear/frightened xxi, 8
Feedback from others 88–9
Feelings xi, xxiii, 8, 9, 13, 23, 29, 30, 56–7, 80–1, 85

'Fight, flight, freeze' response xii, 5
Finances xiv, xv, 10, 58–9, 111
Fists 68–9
Flexibility/adaptability 49, 50–1
Food xv, xxi, 23
Friends, help 11, 19
Friendship xv, xvii, 17, 19, 22, 41, 59
Future, preparing for xiv

Games 21, 66–7
Goal-setting 34–5, 78
'good enough' 34–5, 79, 94
Grades xiii, xviii, 20, 54, 88, 90

Habit, forming new habits ix, x, 36–7, 53, 57, 62, 82, 104–5
Habits, bad 50
Happiness/unhappiness xv, xvii, 16, 22, 32, 56, 84
Happy chemicals 74–5
Harnessing stress xi, xii, xxii, 2–5, 65
Headaches xvii, 8, 68, 96
Health x, xi, xvi, xvii, xviii, xxi, 2, 8, 15, 32, 34, 61, 93, 110, 111
Help, finding support x, xvi, xxii, xxiii, 18–19, 59, 110, 111
Helping others 86–7
Herbal remedies 99

Homesickness xiii, xv, 8, 22–3
Hugs 73
Humour, sense of 8, 24–5

Identity 94, 95
Immune system xvii, xviii, xxi
Impermanence xxii, 12, 13, 81
Independent study xiii, 38
Indigestion 8
International (stress) xv, xvi, 32
International students xv, 111
Introversion 40–2
Irritability 8, 92
Isolation xxi, 8, 40

Jaw-clenching/relaxing 8, 68–9
Joining in 41
Journal 57

Kindness (to self) 22–3, 94–5, 101, 102–3

Laughter 24–5, 68
Lavender 99, 101
Learning xii, xviii, xix, xxi, 50, 88, 89, 98
Lifestyle xiv, xiii, xxiii, 10, 13, 20
Limits, knowing your 34–5, 48–9
Loneliness xxi, xxiii, 8, 40–1

Marks (see Grades)
Massage xxiii, 69, 72, 73, 97, 112
Meditation xxiii, 21, 28, 61
Meeting new people 40–3
Memory xviii, xix, xxi, 20
Mental 'clutter' 26–7, 28–9
Mental health xv, xviii, xxii, 16, 28, 58, 86–7, 111
Migraines xvii, 8
Mind, exposure 66–7
Mindfulness 28–9, 53
Mistakes, making mistakes 88–9, 94
Money (see Finances)
Mood, effect on xviii, 20, 32, 36, 62–3, 66, 98–103
Motivation x, 2, 3, 5
Multi-tasking 69–70
Music 21, 23, 44–5

Names (learning names) 43
Nature xx, 17, 30–3, 45, 61, 99, 112
Negative comparison 95
Nightline 22, 110
'No', saying 34
Nutrition xiv, xv, 10, 59, 62–3, 64, 101, 111

Omega-3 oils 62–3, 99
Option-listing 15, 87
Organised, being well 26–7, 39
Oxytocin xvii, 73, 75

Panic xviii, 77
Panic attacks xviii, 8
'parking' stress 46–7
Perfectionism 39, 89
Personal response xi, xxii, 8–9, 10–13
Perspective 65, 83, 90–1 (see Impermanence)
Physical activity xxi, 16–17, 64, 75, 97, 103, 110
Planner 39
Planning 37, 39, 64–5, 77, 113
Play 84–5, 101
Positive thinking 35, 66, 79, 80, 95
Power naps 21
Pressure xi, xiii, xiv, xv, 9, 38, 76
Prevention, of excess stress 6–9, 34–9, 54, 58, 62, 70
Pride, value of self- 75, 77
Prioritising 13, 39, 71
Problem-solving xii, xviii, 14–15, 46, 47, 50
Progress, tracking x, 106–7

Queues 41

Reality checks 83, 94
Reducing stress xx, 24, 36
Reflection ix, 79
Relationships 10, 18–19
Relaxation exercises 28, 72–3, 96–7
Relaxing xvii, 21, 44–5, 96–103, 112

Resilience xii, xiv, 2–5, 15, 30, 34, 66
Responsibilities xiii
Rest 96
Revising for exams 64–5
Routine, establishing routine 21, 25, 31, 36–7, 48, 49, 53
Breaking routine 50–1

Sadness 92
Samaritans 110, 111
Sanctuary (of calm) 98–9
Scheduling 48–9, 65, 77
Self-awareness ix, 6–13, 94–5
Self-care xxiii, 5, 10–11, 13, 34–5, 64, 95
Self-harming behaviours x, xxiii, 8, 15
Self-worth 86, 94–5
Serotonin xvii, 72, 74, 75
Sharing 54, 55, 59
Signs of stress xvii–xviii, xxiii, xix, xx, 6–9
Singing 43, 44
Sleep xiv, xvi, xvii, xix, xx, xxi, 20–1, 37, 45, 46, 47, 65, 67, 68, 93, 112
Smiling 40, 41
Social exercise 16, 17, 29, 61
Socialising xv, xvii, xxi, 22, 40–1, 75
Social learning 40, 65
Social media 10, 43, 82–3, 99
Social pressures xiv, xv, 40–1

Solution-finding xii, xviii, 14–15, 46, 47, 89, 90–1
Stimulants xxiii, 20, 21, 98, 99
Stress
    Causes of xiii–xiv; xv–xvi, 12, 26–7
    Cycles xix, x
    Effects of prolonged stress xvii–xviii, xxi, xxii
    Excess stress xvii, xviii,
    'Good stress' 2–5
    Inoculation to stress xii, 3
    Physiological response xii, xvii
    Stress balls 69
    'Stress Response' xi, xii, 3, 5
    What is stress? xi, xii
Stressors (see Triggers)
Student lifestyle xiii, xiv, 87
Students and stress xiii, xiv, xv, xviii, xxi, xxii, 54, 64
Student services x
Study, impact of stress xviii, xix–xx, xxi
Study skills 54–5, 64–5, 113

Success xiv, 2
Support x, xvi, xxii, xxiii, 19, 58, 111, 113
Survival mechanism, stress as xii, 46, 93
Symptoms (of stress) xxi, xvii–xviii, xix, xx, 6–9, 24

Tai chi 97, 103
Talking, useful for stress x, xvi, xxiii, 14, 18–19, 61, 91, 92
Task-switching 70–1
Tea 63, 101
Technology 21, 70–1
Teeth-grinding 68
Thinking xviii, 50, 57, 76, 98
    Binary thinking 90
    Thinking time 17
Thought patterns xviii, 9
Threat xii
Time, giving things time 22–3, 61
Time management xiii, xviii, xix, xx, 26–7, 36–7, 38–9, 48–9, 55, 64, 71, 76–7, 113
Tiredness xiii, xix, 3, 8, 10, 20–1, 22, 66, 100–1

Touch, value of 72–3
Triggers 10–11

Uncertainty 9

Values 94, 95
Visualisation 96–7
Volunteering 86–7
Vulnerable, feeling xvii, 98

Walking 17, 21, 31, 60–1
Water 93
Well-being x, xvii–xviii, xxi, 16–17, 20–1, 30–3, 80, 96, 110–12
Winding down 21, 31, 98
Workload xiii, xvi
Worrying xviii, xix, 7, 8, 9, 46–7, 88, 90–1, 102
Writing it down 11, 27, 56–7, 79, 91, 93

Yawning 69
'Yet' 89
Yoga 97

Notes

Notes

Notes

Notes

Notes